THE NEW COMPLETE

MOUNTAIN BIKER

THE NEW C

COMPLETE MOUNTAIN BIKER

Dennis Coello

LYONS & BURFORD PUBLISHERS

Design by MRP Design

Typesetting and composition by CompuDesign

Printed in the United States of America

10 9 8 7 6 5 4 3 2 1

Library of Congress Cataloging-in-Publication Data

Coello, Dennis.
    The new complete mountain biker / Dennis Coello.
        p.   cm.
    Includes index.
    ISBN 1-55821-495-X (pb)
    1. All terrain cycling.   I. Title.
    GV1056.C646   1996
    796.6—DC20   96-42439
                                                              CIP

For Sandy Nieweg

ACKNOWLEDGMENTS

Most of my riding is done solo, but book production is a *group* endeavor. I therefore wish to express my gratitude and indebtedness to:

Lilly Golden, my editor, who brought to the task not only her professional skills but her in-the-saddle knowledge gained as a long-distance touring cyclist;

Ken Gronseth, master bike mechanic and the man completely responsible for the excellent pages in chapter 7 on maintaining front shocks, as well as many of the mechanical insights in that same chapter;

Brad Hansen, another master bike mechanic and general bon vivant, responsible for all the mechanical insights that his friend Ken Gronseth did not provide;

Phil Blomquist (owner of Bicycle Center bike shop in Salt Lake), David Saenz (manager of the Guthrie Bicycle Company bike shop in Salt Lake), Steve Jaboor (manager of Bike and Fitness Center bike shop in St. Louis), and their staffs for answering my dozens of questions and later phone queries;

Dennis Nieweg, Mary Perkins, and Kris Peterson for their artwork;

Shimano, SunTour, and Cannondale for permission to reprint their mechanical drawings;

Jeremy Maue (the boy pictured in chapter 7 fixing a flat) for his patience as I photographed him during the repair that would have taken half the time if I hadn't been around;

and all my fellow riders and bike models who appear on these pages and who somehow maintained their composure when I asked them to pedal a trail "one more time" so I could get a good shot.

Finally, I wish to say a special thanks to Sandy Nieweg, my tireless office assistant and bike model, who somehow manages to perform these tasks in addition to a full-time job. I've dedicated this book to her in part because of her invaluable assistance, but more because she represents the millions of other Americans who over the past two decades have learned the joys of mountain biking.

CONTENTS

INTRODUCTION

This is a book for beginners. It's short, simple, and filled with pictures—a combination designed to answer quickly, or at least as painlessly as possible, the many questions that beset everyone who wishes to begin mountain biking. Questions like:

Which bike do I buy?
Do I need a suspension fork? Rear suspension? Both?
Which is the best gear-changing system?
What kind of equipment do I need for commuting and trail riding?
Can I tour on a mountain bike, or do I need a thin-tire bike for long pavement rides?

You'll find straightforward answers to these questions and many others in the pages that follow. Additional chapters will teach you how to climb and descend steep hills, how to avoid trail obstacles and hop curbs, and how to repair your bike when a flat tire or broken gear cable threatens to strand you across town or in the backcountry.

This expanded and thoroughly rewritten edition of *The Complete Mountain Biker* is designed also to guide the newcomer through the confusion of all the wonderful (and some not-so-workable) advances in bikes and gear over the past few years. But this doesn't mean you'll find a compendium of product reviews. Even bike magazines have difficulty keeping up with all the new offerings in this fast-changing and very technical field, and detailed reviews are too confusing for beginners. They're even confusing for some of us who've been in the saddle for a long time. You may have to be an engineer to understand *why* a particular bike works the way it does, but you only have to be human to love the way it *rides*. This book, in short, is written for those of us who would rather pedal the trails than study the intricacies of our bottom brackets.

Like millions of fellow fat-tire commuters, I pedal city streets in all four seasons. And because I've had the good fortune to make a living through my writing and photography, I often test bikes and gear for cycle companies and magazines. All of this enables me to help make mountain biking a bit less confusing for the beginner.

I welcome you, therefore, to an overview of what kind of riding is possible on mountain bikes, and the kind of bike and components and gear you'll need to have a blast doing it. I've had the pleasure of over twenty years of mountain biking throughout the world. I've pedaled across North America, passed glaciers in Iceland and New Zealand, lost my helmet—momentarily —to monkeys in Bali, shared the dirt roads with plodding water buffalo in China and India, and, in short, enjoyed a thousand places and sights on five continents I'd never have experienced if I'd been forced to remain in the paved-road world. So read on, buy a bike, learn to maintain it, have fun, and accept my hearty wishes for a long and eventful lifetime of two-wheeled explorations.

—Dennis Coello
St. Louis, 1997

1

SELECTING A BIKE

It isn't easy. Choosing the bike that best fits your pocketbook and riding desires is in my mind the single most difficult part of the entire mountain bike experience. It's far tougher than learning to jump logs or climb steep single-track. You only have to walk into a bike shop to see scores of good-looking mounts that at first glance look very much the same.

So yes, choosing your bike is a tough decision. But you're not alone. There are some twelve to fifteen million bikes sold each year in the United States, and roughly 80 percent of those millions are mountain bikes. With such a huge market it's understandable that bike companies galore have moved in to capture their share of the sales.

This is good for you, when it comes to price; all the competition keeps costs low and quality high. Five hundred bucks today buys you a *whole* lot more bike than it did ten years ago.

But it's bad when it comes to figuring out which bike to buy; this competition also translates into bike after bike with this or that option at every price point on the scale. And just like when you're buying a computer, or a car, you've got to look closely and learn what you're looking at before you start seeing the differences.

So how do you begin making sense of it all? I suggest starting off by asking yourself two simple questions:

1. What kind of riding do I intend to do?

2. How much money do I have to spend?

Okay, let's work on question one. Most people fall into one of two categories:

a. those who plan solely to ride to work; and

b. those who wish to do a bit of everything—commuting, dirt road and trail riding, and touring.

Knowing the kind of riding you intend to do will narrow the number of bikes to test-ride.

Let's say you've thought this over and for whatever reason have decided you have absolutely no desire to ride trails. Nor are you interested in backcountry (jeep trails or dirt roads) or paved-road touring. All you're interested in, you figure, is the half a buck or so per driven mile you'll save by commuting to work or school on two wheels instead of four, and the very considerable aerobic workout you'll get in place of a half-asleep drive. "Half a buck?!" you say, incredulously. Well, remember this figure includes *all* costs of car ownership—purchase price, insurance, gas, oil, upkeep, parking, et cetera.

At roughly two-hundred-twenty workdays per year, and, say, a fifteen-mile round-trip ride, you'll save—at fifty cents per mile—a whopping $1,650 *annually*. That figure should make the cost of a bike and gear a bit more palatable.

If you say you want a bike for commuting, the bike shop clerk will probably steer you toward a city bike, also called a hybrid—a lower-cost, thinner-tubed (frame tubes, that is) and thinner-tired, higher-geared (lacking

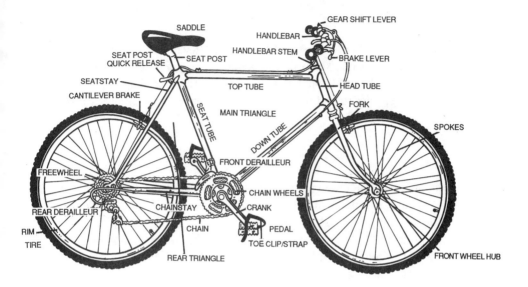

the very-easy-to-pedal low gears, also called granny-gears) and more swept-back handlebarred bike than the meaner-looking mountain bike next to it. The city bike, in fact, will probably remind you of your old thin-tire touring bike, except for the upright handlebars. The salesperson will tell you, truthfully, that you don't need a more expensive full-on mountain bike if all you want to do is pedal pavement back and forth to work.

Presto—you've got a great rig for commuting, you've saved some cash, and you're happy. Until, that is, you happen upon a dirt road or single-track trail and get hooked on off-pavement travel. Or until you change jobs and your new commute is on pavement that is full of potholes and so chewed up that it eats your wheels and jars your fillings loose in a week.

In short, if you're absolutely certain you won't want to do anything but commute, buy a hybrid and use the "Accessories" chapter in this book to help you outfit it—and you—for the road. However, if there's a chance you'll want to do anything beyond commuting with your bike, purchase a true mountain bike. You can redesign it for almost any purpose and all terrains, including fast commuting over any streets this world can throw at you.

Most prospective fat-tire bikers fall into the second category—those who wish to do all kinds of riding, or at least want the option to do so. Knowing this, the bike companies offer a dazzling array of machines. So for you people, let's go through the list of attributes a "real" mountain bike possesses. Once you know these basics you can better understand the subtler differences among bikes—differences that sometimes cost a lot. At the end of this section, and before you walk into a bike shop, you'll have to ask yourself, How much do I want to spend? Then head for the bike shop to take the first of *many* test-rides to find the perfect bike for you within your price range.

■ FRAME ■

Over the years I've pedaled everything from the shiny $250 mounts you see at discount and department stores, to $5,000 beauties on display at international bike shows. The frames of these bikes range in metals from tank-weight steel all the way up to metamic (a boron carbide/aluminum combination). When we're talking frames on a bike, we're talking its *character*. Hang the best components on a no-account frame and the bike is still low class where and when it matters.

Mountain bike frames are made of one or more of the following materials:

- Steel
- Chro-moly steel alloy
- Composite-fiber
- Aluminum
- Titanium
- Metamic, etc.

Take your business elsewhere if someone offers a great deal on some straight-gauge, steel-throughout frame—that makes the bike tip the scales in the mid-to-high thirties (pounds)—or you'll be walking the beast up plenty of hills later on. Just as bad is the fact that these sluggish bikes provide a dead-horse feel whenever you're in the saddle. And unless you've got a real wad to drop, you'll bypass the pricey composite-fiber frames and titanium, metamic, and other twenty-first-century metals.

The frame tubes of most mountain bikes you'll find in the shops are made either of one of several aluminums or a type of steel alloy called chrome-molybdenum ("chro-moly," "chro-mo steel," or "chro-mo"). Chances are if you are looking at bikes selling for five hundred and up you won't find any frames made of the less expensive and far heavier steel sometimes described as "high-tensile steel" in the catalogs, and occasionally on a down-tube decal. Some bikes in that range might choose to hang a better grade of components or saddle and handlebars than their competitors, offsetting the cost by offering frames whose "main-triangle" tubes (the down, top, and seat tubes) are chro-mo but whose fork, chainstay, and seatstay tubes are the heavy high-tensile. This isn't bad, necessarily, but you ought to know what you're buying. If you're looking for a bike in a lower price range, ask for a bike with the chro-moly main triangle without the fancy components. I don't want you to be unimpressed when you see a decal or read a specification (spec) chart boasting a frame made of "Reynolds 753 chro-moly." I also don't want you to be confused when you're in a high-end store and salespeople describe some eight-hundred-dollar beauty as "steel." At this price they're talking *chro-mo* steel—the good kind—but to be safe, ask for confirmation.

You might also see the word "butted," or "double-butted," or even "triple-butted" (all variations on the thickness of the butting) on decals and in the spec charts of bike company catalogs. This refers to a huge leap up in quality from straight-gauge steel tubing; butting allows both greater strength and lighter weight. Butted tubes are like our bones: thinner-walled in the middle, and thicker toward the ends where stress is greatest.

Another thing to look for in a frame is the weld points. They should be clean, uniform, and free of pinholes.

Suspension

Now we come to the subject of *suspension,* a relatively recent addition to mountain bikes that serves a purpose not unlike a shock absorber in a car. In the shops you'll see some bikes with large accordionlike black rubber boots or other suspension gadgetry on or above the fork, and other bikes with large coiled springs or hingelike accoutrements near the rear wheel. The coming of suspension to the mountain bike world has spawned new terminology: "rigid" bikes, meaning those with no suspension; "hardtails," referring to those with front suspension only; and "full-suspension," for those with both suspended front and rear. If you encourage the usually knowledgeable bike shop folks, you're likely also to hear of Horst links, rocker arms, linkage designs, high-, mid-, low-, and high–low pivot points, and URTs (unified rear triangles, where the bottom bracket moves when the rear wheel is compressed). So for heaven's sake, don't encourage them.

Your immediate question is, of course, do I need a bike with suspension? Again, the answer lies in your response to the two questions of how and where you'll ride, and how much you want to spend.

Test-ride all three kinds of frames (rigids, hardtails, full-suspension), even on pavement (most bike shops won't appreciate you hammering down a trail on their mounts), and you'll probably get hooked on the silky smooth feel of suspension. Many people rule out rear suspension because of the additional cost, but love the omission of "chatter" (vibration transmitted through the handlebars) through the far less costly front suspension. Commuters have little call for front or rear suspension; hard-core trail riders usually want front or full suspension; backcountry and pavement tourers who want to pack front panniers are still waiting for a rack that can be mounted securely to a bike with fork (front) suspension.

There are some, however, who choose not to follow these trends. Me, for example. Those of us who still pedal rigids generally do so for one or more of the following reasons: (1) weight—nonsuspended mountain bikes can be as light as road bikes, while front suspension generally adds a pound to the frame, and full suspension adds even more; (2) price—yes, you'll find some front-suspension bikes for the same price as rigids, but look more closely and you'll see that the manufacturer made up the difference through lower-cost components or similar cost savings somewhere else on the bike; (3) the "direct-connection" feel of the road or trail provided only by a rigid; (4) suspension means one more thing you've got to service now and again; (5) suspension forks or frames sell to many because they look neat, but if you're rarely on rough trails it's hard to justify the extra weight and cost.

Fortunately, there's a middle ground for those buyers who think they'll want front or even full suspension in future, but don't have the necessary bucks today. Many companies now offer suspension-ready frames on midrange and higher-cost bikes, which means they're built with tube-angle geometry that will accept front suspension when you can afford a new fork down the road. The rear suspension can come from the addition of something like the K.E.I. Hydra Post Seat Post Shock Absorber. I've never tested one myself, but I imagine it's like riding atop a large spring. At present my knees and elbows are sufficient suspension for my style of riding, but I'll sign up when they give out.

Now that you know about frame material options and suspension, compare oranges with oranges. If you're choosing between a bike with butted chro-mo steel throughout (all tubes are high quality) and one of aluminum, you'll find that during a test-ride aluminum is far stiffer, speedier, and more responsive, and that a chro-mo steel frame gives a gentler ride. (Keep in mind that the size and inflation of your tires can have a lot to do with how stiff a ride you'll have.) Because steel is more flexible and because it's somewhat less expensive, two-thirds of all shock-free (nonsuspension) bikes are steel. All of which would argue in favor of steel for those bikers who expect to tour on their mounts (less vibration that might be bothersome hour after hour), and aluminum for those who wish a snappier feel on the trail. I prefer the responsiveness of aluminum, and I tour for months of every year.

What a test-ride won't tell you is that repairs to steel frames are *much* less expensive than those to aluminum frames, and because the metal is less brittle repairs are required less often. (Some companies warranty their steel frames for life, their aluminum frames for three to five years.)

Now that you know the steel/aluminum argument, and realize that with some bikes there are only shades of difference between the metals, you'll understand the need to set aside some time to test-ride bikes in a thoughtful manner. (Worse yet, there are even nuances of difference in stiffness among different aluminums; expect 6000-series tubes to be more resilient than the stiffer, harsher-riding 7000. In general you'll find that smaller-tubed/ thicker-walled aluminum frames provide softer rides than the larger-tubed/ thinner-walled aluminum.) Show up at the shop with a small notebook and a pen, and record your impressions and comparisons. Visit a second shop to test the brands it carries, and whatever you do be patient before you buy. You'll appreciate it later.

By the way, if you're height deprived you shouldn't be surprised if you're steered toward steel in the bike shop. The reason is that smaller aluminum frames are thought to transmit too much road and trail shock to the rider; more of this shock is dissipated when traveling through longer-tubed frames. Cannondale, however, offers some of its smallest bikes with front or full suspension, so if test-rides on aluminum rigids prove to be too harsh and you want to stick with aluminum, there is a solution.

Two additional items you might notice on the frame are *replaceable dropouts* (where the wheel axle fits into the frame) and *derailleur hangers* (the piece of the frame to which the derailleur is attached). Very rough trail riding can cause problems in these two areas (more generally with a bent derailleur hanger); look for them on aluminum frames, and recognize they're less important with steel. Bang up most aluminum frames and you're simply out of luck, so you can see the value of replaceable parts—*if* your riding style requires it.

I've included information on frame construction and geometry at the end of this chapter for those who want to know more, but what you've read thus far should be sufficient preparation to begin your preliminary search. I'm a believer in buying the best that you can but not more than you need. No matter what kind of riding you do you'll enjoy a good, solid, lightweight frame. My final suggestion is that you remain bikeless till you can afford at least to bypass the heavy low-grade clunkers. You can always upgrade the rest of your bike later on. Bikes are like our bodies: We can build up muscle and reduce cholesterol, but there's not a whole lot we can do to improve the bones we get from the beginning.

> Note: Female riders should read closely the *Bike Fit* and *Women's Frames* sections beginning on page 22 before choosing a frame, for even some titanium sweetheart of a bike will prove a passing fancy if it doesn't fit perfectly.

▪ DRIVETRAIN ▪

Thankfully your bike's drivetrain has a lot fewer parts than the one in your car. A bike's 'train consists of *shifters, front derailleur, rear derailleur, crankset, cogs,* and *chain*. Pick up a bike with a poorly functioning drive-train and, no matter how good the frame, you're not going to be interested in developing the relationship.

Shifters have changed so dramatically over the years as to almost have come full circle. More than three decades ago I took my first cross-country ride on a three-speed bike that had a nifty twist-grip shifter at the right hand. Today the rage is Grip Shift, almost exactly what I enjoyed all those years ago. Now, however, there are twenty-four gears attached.

Shifting mechanisms for mountain bikes come in three styles:

1. The Grip Shift.
2. Above the bar, an example of which is the Shimano SIS (Shimano Index Shifting).
3. Below the bar, an example of which is the Shimano Alvio.

Index, or "click," shifting has entirely replaced friction-mode shifters. The difference between them is that the index shifters click into place for each gear, automatically positioning the derailleur above the desired cog front and rear.

Grip Shift   Above the bar shifter

Below the bar shifter

Index shifter lever set on friction option.

My problem with index shifting is that I've yet to find a system as simple and relatively maintenance-free as is friction. Which is why, whenever I'm buying the current model of click shifter on a new bike, I make certain it has a friction option. Like the manual-option override setting on an automatic camera, it will get you by when the newer doodads go out of adjustment. In addition, while the current breed of Grip Shift is better than the first edition, I find it to be more sensitive to mud and crud and definitely more difficult when it comes to cable replacement. Gore-Tex/Teflon cables and housings help to counteract this problem, but this is a pricey solution if you're paying full retail.

And then there's the fact that I *like* friction shifting. I like being able to hit exactly the gear I want because of my history with a particular bike. If I were a racer, of course, the efficiency of the shifter would mean everything; performance would be critical. But biking for me is a mixture of pleasure and performance. And just as there's pleasure to be derived from manually shifting a finely tuned automobile as you take a few miles of curves and hills, there's pleasure, too, in friction shifting your way along single-track.

On another matter, whatever kind of shifter you have must be located where you can reach it easily. That's no problem with Grip Shift, since your hand is at or near the bar end anyway. And it's no problem with independently mounted shifters, in which the shifter assembly and brake lever are separate. This allows a large-handed rider, like myself, to distance the shifter from the bar end; smaller-handed cyclists decrease this distance for perfect alignment with the thumb. But some shifters—like the old Shimano Exage line—came as a single-piece brake lever/thumb shifter. The rider was required to conform to the bike, not the other way around. Exage has passed, as it should have, but be on the lookout for these kinds of seemingly insignificant characteristics.

One feature of some of the shifting systems that I thoroughly do not like is the inability to shift more than a single gear at a time. Be sure that your test-rides are long enough to allow a comfortable feeling with the derailleur controls, comfortable enough to determine if you'll like the system after you get the hang of it. The tendency is to think you'll like something more once you've used it for a while, but the multilevered ratchet shifting required with some systems (like the currently popular—though not user-serviceable, unless of course you split atoms at your day job—Shimano Rapidfire Plus, in which you have a thumb lever and an index-finger-activated lever) makes me feel like I'm pumping a well when I need to switch more than one gear at a time. My old SIS/friction-option system does not require multiple hand motions for multigear upshifts; nor does Grip Shift. With Grip Shift, however, it's awfully hard to brake and downshift at the same time. And that's a pain because you'll want to shift into an easier gear when you stop (it makes taking off again so much easier). Yes, you can get used to it and learn to remember to shift before you have to brake. But with my above-the-bar-mounted thumb-control shifter I can brake and downshift at the same time, something I find very useful, especially when commuting.

▪ BRAKES ▪

There are three requirements in this department: (a) good stopping power; (b) levers that are easy to reach, quick to engage, and which feel good to the hand; and (c) brakes that are easy to adjust, at both the lever (for in-the-saddle adjustments) and the rim.

Now, it's easy to determine the first of these requirements during test-rides: Just ask to ride a bike with high-quality brakes (like the Shimano STX-RC), and compare the stopping power of all other brakes to these. You don't want to get a test bike dirty, but pedaling through a puddle will give you an idea also of the critical *wet* stopping power of brakes and pads. (I make

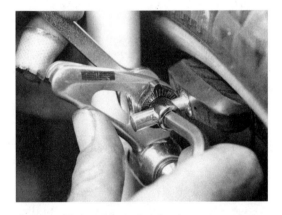

Break pad being adjusted at the rim.

it a habit to carry a shop cloth—one of those red washable rags you see in abundance in auto repair shops—in a fanny pack when I test-ride bikes. This allows me to wipe down the bike before I return it to the shop. Remember, you want the salesperson and the mechanic of your neighborhood bike shop to work *with* you at finding the best bike for your needs, not wince each time they see you walk in the door.)

The second requirement of good brakes is almost as easy to determine as the first—the snappy, sure feel of a great lever in the hand is obvious from the start. There should be very little lever wobble, and if the shop has done a credible job of building the bike, the pads will be aligned on the rim surface (not hitting the rim at an angle, or resting against the rim at a point above or below the rim surface).

No brake lever will feel good to the hand, however, nor will it engage the braking action quickly or cleanly, if it isn't within easy reach while your thumb remains hooked securely around the bar. For safety's sake, check for this while still in the store, before your test-ride, and ask if whatever brake model you're looking at has adjustable-reach settings. If so, the salesperson shouldn't mind resetting it before you hit the streets: If you can't reach the brakes, there's a good chance the store will have lost both a customer and a bike.

The third requirement, however—that of brakes being easy to adjust—is not a simple matter to determine. Yes, you can try the in-the-saddle adjustment at the lever (as long as you reset it before returning it to the shop), but you should not begin tweaking the brakes themselves with an Allen wrench during a test-ride. For that matter, you shouldn't begin messing around with brakes even on a bike that you own until you've reviewed the process in this book (chapter 7), in the instruction sheets that often come from the component manufacturer, or in another bike mechanics book. Unless, of course, you're lucky enough to be admitted into that exclusive sanctum of the bike shop mechanic's lair, and have the opportunity to be taught by the very wrench him- or herself.

Cantilevered brakes.

So while you can't in good conscience start fiddling with the brakes to determine how easily they can be adjusted, you *can* ask the salesperson how to go about it. And how easy it is compared to the brakes on other models.

Finally, just as with brakes, all brake pads are not created equal. If you know you're testing top-of-the-line cantilevers, or center-pulls (the kind of brake you'll find on almost all mountain bikes at present), but still aren't satisfied with the stopping power, the answer may lie in one of the excellent aftermarket pads available through catalogs and in some good bike shops.

▪ WHEELS AND TIRES ▪

Don't get too hung up on "box construction" or other terms when it comes to finding high-quality wheels. Most bikes in the mid- to higher range will come fitted with amazingly strong cassette hub–equipped wheels that are light in weight and capable of handling everything from the monster off-road 2.2-inch Specialized Cannibals to my favorites for fast city commutes and touring—the Avocet Cross (with internal tread) or Performance Fast City STK, both at a narrow 1.25 inches. (If you expect to do a lot of commuting I strongly suggest you consider paying the extra dollars for Kevlar-belted tires. Kevlar is the material used in many law-enforcement protective vests. If it can repel rounds, it can surely help to ward off punctures from glass and thorns.)

The time to discuss which tires you'll need—knobbies or slicks—is when you buy your bike, when for a nominal fee the salesperson will probably swap tires for you. Most of us will be happy with the trail-running rubber that comes standard on the bike, but if you know you'll spend most of your time commuting or touring, then there's no sense in buying a set of tires designed for another task. For a more detailed discussion on tires, see page 39.

When buying a bike, be sure its wheels are made of an aluminum alloy—not steel. Steel wheels and gumwall tires will be found only on very inexpensive bikes, and, combined, add weight that will make your cycling *much* more difficult. An extra ounce on your wheel affects you much more than an extra ounce on your bike frame or on you. This is because heavy wheels greatly increase your "rolling weight," the weight that not only must be propelled linearly down the road or trail, but must also be "rolled" around and around.

A good argument can be made against quick-release wheels on mountain bikes. Fail to align the quick-release (q-r) levers with the fork and chainstay, I've heard and read, and you run the risk of flipping open the lever when riding off-road. And then there's the far more real possibility of losing a front wheel to a thief when you've locked only the frame of your bike in town.

But I still prefer quick-release wheels, front and back, for convenience sake. I've never unintentionally opened a q-r lever, in all my years of trail riding. And as for warding off thieves, make sure you lock your wheels securely to your bike with a heavy chain or one of the many long-shackle U-locks.

Finally, there's the choice of Presta or Schrader valve stems. Most high-performance bikes these days come with wheels drilled out for Presta valves, which are thinner than the automobile-type Schraders. Which is better? Again, it depends. Many people prefer Presta because they are activated by

Schrader valve

Presta valve

air pressure alone, as this makes them a bit easier to inflate. I like them for their nicely machined metal, and for the small round threaded nut that secures the valve in place against the rim. The wider Schrader valve stems look clunky in comparison, are air-and-spring-pressure activated, and are rubber rather than metal. As a result they must be mounted carefully; if they aren't straight they'll rub against the metal of the rim hole and produce a flat that cannot be patched.

All this argues against Schrader valves, and yet I prefer them. I even drilled out the Presta-sized holes in the second set of wheels I bought for my mountain bike so that I could run with Schraders only. The reasons? Because while Prestas are easier to pump up, I find them not all that much easier. So that point's a wash. Next, although I admire the machined metal valve, I don't like having to unscrew the tiny delicate stem (that rests above it) to inflate the tube; Schraders in contrast are pure simplicity. Yes, you have to make sure the Schrader stem is perpendicular to the rim when replacing it, but that's like remembering to tie your shoes. So none of these "advantages" I hear hyped by many riders begins to overcome the single greatest disadvantage that bothers me: You can't pop into a filling station to air up (carefully!) with their hose without hassling with an adapter.

Some riders keep an adapter in place always (though when I tried this they unscrewed after many miles and fell off), and while I pack an adapter in my tool bag (just in case I come upon a rider who needs a shot of air and doesn't have one to fit my hand pump), I don't want to have to dig for it when popping in for air. And while I've read and been told that the slightly larger hole in a rim drilled for a Schrader is structurally less sound, in three decades of piling an amazing amount of weight upon all manner of Schrader valve rims, I've yet to crumple one. Even when I load them with eighty pounds of winter touring gear on me.

▪ SEALED BEARINGS ▪

I doubt there's a mountain bike born these days with unsealed bearings, but in case you see "sealed" in the literature I'll explain it. Until mountain bikes came about, wheel and bottom bracket bearings were protected from the elements by only tight-fitting metal caps and whatever grease you'd packed over the balls the last time you pulled maintenance.

With all the grit and grime of off-road and dirt-road biking, however, further bearing protection was essential. And so the elves got busy designing rubber flaps and sleeves and other ways by which to shield your bearings from the elements. "Shielded" would be a better term than "sealed," by the way; while there are some systems that are truly sealed (and therefore not rider-serviceable), almost all mountain bike bearings are water- and grit-*resistant,* not water- and grit-*proof.* Which means that while you can pull maintenance on them less often, you can't just forget about it forever.

Three types of handlebar ends.

▪ HANDLEBARS ▪

Before looking for a bar that's comfortable, make sure you're testing a bike that fits you well. A good shop will make sure of this before you head out the door. Many of the city or hybrid bikes come equipped with perfectly flat bars, assuming perhaps that you'll most often be riding in a completely upright position. Real mountain biking, however—and by that I mean fun cycling over any kind of terrain—usually involves anything but single-position saddle sitting. And so you'll find a host of choices: some bars that are perfectly flat, but more that angle up and back, up and forward, that curve down a bit like short roadie handlebars. Most handlebars are much shorter in width than those gracing the early mountain bikes, but you'll find long and short stems, stems that rise at sharp and shallow angles, and bar "end" attachments of many different lengths and shapes (and all of these adapters are excellent for improving your climbing power as well as providing additional riding positions for your hands). You'll soon find one handlebar that feels better than the rest when you're in the saddle. If the bike of your dreams doesn't come with bar ends in place, I suggest you add them immediately.

And don't let the shop attendants cut the bar ends down to what they'll tell you is "normal length." You can do this later yourself with a hacksaw once you've determined the length you prefer, or return to the shop and they'll do it for you. I say this because I prefer handlebars with very long bar ends that reach forward and then curve inward. These provide various grip-holds that allow me to climb, to cruise while leaning farther forward than the bars alone would allow (and thus to increase my power to the pedals, because more torque can be applied whenever you lean forward), and to stretch far out over the bars during those long straight miles into a head wind. You know, like being in the drops on thin-tire touring bikes, but this is better, because your body is not in some paperclip-type curl, with your neck straining to support your head as you tilt it up to see where you're going.

Also, make sure you know what you're buying when it comes to bars and bar ends. Remember what you've learned about frame-tube materials. Bars and bar ends are tubes too, after all, and they come in lovely chro-mo steel and aluminum—and in not-so-lightweight metals as well. Also, don't let yourself be turned off good handlebars and bar ends because they're sheathed in lousy grips. Slap on a pair of high-quality Scott, Pedro, Ritchey, or other grips and you'll notice an amazing difference in feel and control.

▪ SEATPOST ▪

This is another tube, so be sure you know what it's made of, although you can always replace it later with a lighter chro-moly or aluminum model. Next, check its length. Technical riders will want to purchase as small a frame as possible, for the increased maneuverability, and compensate with a long seatpost—which means somewhere in the 320 mm to 350 mm range. (If you do this, be sure also that your handlebar stem length is sufficient to be raised—safely— to the height you'll need to take it.) Because I prefer smoother, nontechnical, single-track, and dirt-road riding, I like a larger frame. And because I do a great deal

Seatpost with quick release lever.

of commuting and paved-road touring on my mountain bike, I want as large a frame as will fit me. Why? Because I want plenty of room for multiple water-bottle mounts and panniers.

Make sure the seatpost quick-release lever doesn't perform major surgery on your thigh when you pedal. Blood is something you definitely want to avoid while mountain biking.

▪ PEDALS ▪

Yep, you guessed it. They come in both lousy (heavy but cheap) and good (strong and lightweight) steel alloy. Some also come with elements of both. If you can afford all alloy, buy it. Even better (and lighter) are the alloy cage and body pedals, with a chro-moly axle (a pedal axle is also called a spindle). Good mountain bike pedals are also sealed to the elements with rubber seals repelling the muck.

You'll also have to decide if you want the toe-clip-and-strap model or the clipless style. The latter weighs less but requires you to pedal in shoes designed to engage the clips. Commuters, tourers, and those looking more for adventure in the saddle than for performance and speed usually opt for toe clips and straps. While recent clipless shoe models are more comfortable when out of the saddle and won't make you look like a duck while walking about, they still aren't for me. On a recent tour through Holland I watched, and waited, while my clipless tourmates changed shoes every time they saddled up. And while you do indeed have greater pedal control with clipless shoes, and gain greater power on the upstroke, neither benefit to me is worth the hassle. Or the noise. Begin a ride in a pack of clipless wonders and you'll hear what sounds like a dozen angry lobsters clacking their claws.

▪ BRAZE-ONS ▪

Pay attention as well to the presence or lack of "braze-ons"—water-bottle mounts, cable guides, rack and fender eyelets. Many trail riders want—and need—three water-bottle mounts (the third fits beneath the down tube). The placement of these braze-ons is also important: you don't want one of them digging into your shoulder or back when portaging your bike. Test for this by lifting the bike upon your shoulder while in the bike shop or during your test-ride. (For the proper way to portage a bike, see chapter 3.)

Double eyelets in back are a must for commuters, since you'll need a rack for a bag of some kind, plus a second set of eyelets to attach full-wrap fenders. In the next chapter I'll tell you of some great lightweight plastic fenders that require no eyelets for attachment, but even these beauties allow too much spray if you're riding to work. For commuting there's no getting around full-wrap fenders. Making a single rack-mounting bolt do the double duty of supporting both the rack and fender stays greatly weakens the bolt's ability to support the weight you'll pile on the rack when stopping "for a few things at the grocery" on the way home. While some racks offer fender-stay mounting points, they generally offer only a single attachment point on each side, and full-wrap fenders require two stays on either side of the wheel.

▪ CRANKARM LENGTH ▪

Crankarms (commonly referred to simply as cranks) are the long metal shafts between the bottom bracket and pedals. It stands to reason that the longer the crank, the greater leverage or torque you'll be able to apply. Imagine a large nut in place of your bottom bracket, and your crankarms as wrenches (to which you've applied your feet instead of hands—with toe clips and straps or clipless pedals to provide the grip that your fingers would otherwise allow). Suddenly you'd like the longest crank you can find, right? Unfortunately, as with almost all aspects of cycling, and with life, we soon approach the realm of required compromise. Make your cranks too long and they'll eat the dirt. And so will you.

Many cranks still hover at 170 mm, a fine length for thin-tire touring bikes but unnecessarily short for the standard high-bottom brackets required on mountain bikes to get you over obstacles on the trail. More and more commonly seen on mountain bikes are 175-mm crankarms, but very long-legged riders might consider swapping for 180 mm on custom frames.

▪ GEAR SPREAD ▪

It used to be that almost every mountain bike came with the stock gears of a 28/38/48 *crankset* (the three *chain rings,* the numbers derived from the number of teeth in each sprocket), and a 14–30 *freewheel,* or *cluster* at the rear axle (six or seven sprockets ranging from fourteen teeth in the smallest to thirty in the largest). Now most clusters have either seven or eight cogs. The resulting gear-inch range (this term and its derivation are explained on page 29) was 24–89. For now it is enough to know that the lower number refers to the easiest pedaling possible with this particular gear arrangement; 89 is the hardest. To translate the 24–89 range to a three-speed manual-transmission automobile, think of first gear (your lowest gear, the one you use to pull hills) as the 24 number, and third gear as 89. My own views on gearing run in the opposite direction of where the bike builders of the world are headed. Which means when I buy a bike I have to alter the gears (change the chain rings or change one or more of the cogs in the freewheel, or both) to get the range I prefer. My problem with the 24–89 range was that I found it insufficiently wide; there was no low gear low enough for me to pedal up steep trails and dirt roads when packing panniers, and no high gear high enough to let me take advantage of those wind-at-the-back days on tour when my tires were eating up the hard dirt roads or pavement, or when I needed speed on my commutes to keep from being late for work. Because I wanted to do all my trail riding, commuting, and touring on the same bike, I needed to expand my gear range.

So I changed things. I replaced the smallest chain ring, the 28-tooth, with a 24-tooth. And I replaced the 14–30 cluster with sprockets ranging between 13 and 34. This gave me the range of 18–96. I found it low enough for climbing dirt even with fairly heavy loads, but insufficiently high when using high-pressure slicks on pavement. So I returned to my 26-inch (wheel size) gear chart (like the one you'll find in the appendix, page 217) and saw that if I dropped from a 13-tooth smallest freewheel cog to a 12 I'd have a whopping 104-inch gear, almost as high as I have on the touring bike that collects dust leaning against the wall in my bedroom. Alternatively, I could have increased the size of my largest chain ring and left the freewheel alone, for this too would have provided me with a higher gear. I leaned toward the option of reducing the metal on my bike, rather than increasing it. But on the other side of the equation was the fact that the smaller the cog, the faster it wears out. It was, again, trade-off time. I chose the smaller freewheel cog. And everything worked like a charm because I had a rear derailleur that could throw a chain across that wide a range of cogs. Now I make the gear change part of the deal at the time of sale, unless I have the necessary cogs and chain rings lying about at home. Which means you can do the same *if* you decide you want a range like mine.

The industry is just now beginning to offer 22-tooth chain rings on some bikes, a lovely step toward easier climbs. But in the battle to offer lighter and lighter bikes, many companies have *decreased* the largest (easiest) cog in the freewheel, thus reducing the benefits of the smaller chain ring. (This gets confusing, and will remain so until you read the lengthy explanation later in this chapter and study your bike for a minute. In short, as the sprockets get bigger in front, the gears get higher. As they get bigger in back, the gears get lower.) Even if you buy a bike with a tiny 22-tooth chain ring, therefore, you're only at a lowest-possible gear of 20.4 when matched with the 28-tooth largest freewheel cog.

The answer? Build your legs to superhuman strength. Or don't mind it when things go funny in your knees. Or, simpler, and far less expensive than surgery, increase the largest freewheel cog to a 30. Do so and your lowest gear drops to 19.1. And if you want even easier pedaling up the steepest of hills, *and* if your derailleur can handle it, bump up another two teeth to a 32.

In the bike shop you'll hear that shifting isn't as smooth across such a wide range, that it will cost you X dollars to make the gear changes, and X dollars more for a derailleur that can handle a freewheel cog increase to a 32 or 34. Is it worth it? Again, it all depends upon the riding you plan to do, and the money you're willing to spend.

See "More on Gearing" on page 29 for more detailed information.

▪ SADDLE ▪

I once began an around-the-world bike tour on a brand-new, all-leather Brooks Professional saddle. My lord, the pain. It's not that I was so stupid that I didn't know to break it in first. There just wasn't the time to do it, what with working and completing finals and saying good-bye to everyone. But for those first two weeks, two *long* weeks in a hard saddle, I cursed myself for not making the time.

I mention that painful memory so that you'll know that "saddle-sore" is a term applicable not only to cowboys. Thankfully, many of today's saddles are amazingly comfortable at the start, unlike the hard-as-rocks, all-leather beauties that take time to soften and conform to your derriere. Manufacturers often shave the overall cost of a showroom bike by offering a less-than-superb saddle. The difference between good and bad is difficult to see, but

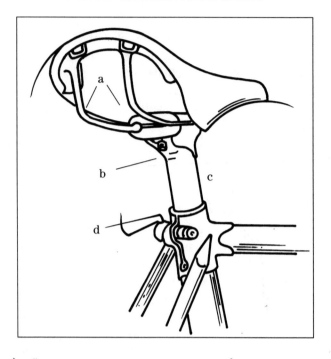

a) rails   ***c)*** seatpost
b) Allen head adjustment bolt   ***d)*** quick-release lever

test-rides will give you a hint of what might be comfortable. As the sales-person to show you other saddles and let you know how they compare with what comes stock.

Aside from the issue of comfort, which can be satisfied by shape, size, and material (gel or closed-cell foam or other interior, usually covered by thin leather or Lycra), there is the question of weight. And therefore the question, once again, of dollars. You'll have a choice between good and bad steel rails (the two long metal rods running beneath the saddle to attach to the seatpost; the saddle is adjusted along these rails to fine-tune the distance between you and the handlebars), or the far more expensive and far lighter titanium option.

▪ BIKE FIT ▪

It is unfortunately true that most people think only in terms of height when it comes to choosing a bike that fits. Chances are good that they'll purchase a bike that fits their leg length, but whether it also matches their upper-torso and arm length is another matter. And while few good bike shops these days will fail to match the entire human with the proper machine, it's still a good idea to know what to look for.

Height

When straddling a bike I like an inch of clearance over the top tube on thin-tire touring bikes, and between two and four inches of clearance on ATBs. Commuters and tourers will tend toward less clearance; hard-core trail riders want four and sometimes more between them and the bar. I stick with a two-inch clearance, since I prefer to do all three kinds of riding on a single bike, and simply take a little more care on the trails.

So the only real opportunity to foul up when it comes to height is to fail to wear the shoes with the same level heel as the kind you ride in when you head to the bike shop. And remember my words on obtaining a long seatpost.

Length

Not many people have spent much time thinking about how *long* a bike should be. But hop aboard one that's way wrong for you and you'll know it very soon. You'll be stretched out uncomfortably to reach the handlebars and pain will come in your back and neck. If it's too short you'll find your hands wanting to reach beyond the bars, your elbows bent like wings, and your body too far forward to add the power gained when pulling the handlebars toward you to tackle hills.

So what's the proper length? It's what you find comfortable—within the realm of what will work for your riding style. For example, commuters usually prefer a more upright, good-view-of-the-traffic position in the saddle than do trail riders, though they also need to be able to tuck and pedal hard when late for work or escaping a truck. A straight-backed, George-Washington-in-the-saddle pose will rob you of leg power as well as almost all upper-torso muscle power. Buy the right-sized bike for you, with a long seatpost and bar ends, and you'll be able to change your position in the saddle and the degree to which you lean forward whenever you wish.

Some shops have their own methods of measuring buyers for bikes, but most will have you straddle a bike to determine height, then sit in the saddle and lean forward to determine proper length. Some watch for an easy reach to the grips, elbows bent slightly, and the middle of the knee direct-ly over the pedal when the foot (and pedal) are at three o'clock. Others will drop a plumb line from the rider's nose, making sure it lands a half inch or so behind the handlebars. If the bike shop leaves the matter of a proper bike fit completely up to you, you should try another shop.

Women's Frames

Most women have proportionately shorter torsos and arms than men, but somewhat longer legs. Back in the dark ages of one-size-fits-all frames (not so many years ago), women would therefore often find that bikes that fit them perfectly in height did not fit them in terms of length. The top tube (running from the seatpost to the head tube) was just too long. Thankfully, many bike companies have now responded to the very large female segment of the market by offering bikes with shorter top tubes and stems.

There are still a few companies that beat the height problem by setting their frames on top of 24-inch wheels. The problem here is that mountain biking is almost exclusively a 26-inch world, making tires and tubes and rim strips hard to find when you're on tour and have run through all your spares. But if you don't anticipate world rides on the bike, and if no other frame feels right, this might be the answer.

Another problem still facing some shorter women is the difficulty in obtaining a bike in which the handlebars rest at the usually preferred level of the saddle height. Given the 26-inch wheel, the height of a large knobby tire and the required mud-clearance distance between it and the fork crown, a standard-height head tube, the usual slightly rising stem, and the vertical space added by a suspension fork, the total height often puts the handlebars in the uncomfortable riding position above the saddle. It's like sitting at the dinner table on a chair that's too low. Well, it's taken a while, but the industry has at last responded with stems that have a zero-degree or even a negative rise. Women riders, continue to look around to find a bike that fits *properly*. You will, after all, be paying full-sized dollars for what you buy.

Other elements for women riders to consider are saddles designed specifically for them, shorter crankarms, small-diameter grips and short-reach brake handles, and narrow handlebars. Grip Shift shifting might be preferable for some women who find thumb- or thumb/finger-lever opera-tions difficult due to smaller hands. Remember that chro-moly steel is the generally preferred metal for small frames, due to the road shock transmitted through small aluminum framesets. But if you like the stiffer ride that any aluminum provides, remember, too, that there are softer- and harsher-riding aluminum frames of exactly the same size, depending upon tube size and construction methods. Or you could drop the bucks for the answer to this problem offered by that venerable aluminum frame builder Cannondale—full-suspension, very small frames.

Kids' Frames

Full-on, triple-chain-ring mountain bikes for kids is a growing market, and companies have responded not only with the lower-grade and heavier high-tensile steel most commonly seen in kids' bikes, but with full chromoly as well. Wheel sizes of 20 inches, 24 inches, and 26 inches are offered, but parents should keep in mind the fact that the smaller the wheel, the more difficult it is to roll over obstacles. If you have the choice of a larger wheel size on the same size frame, choose it.

Buy a bike that fits *now.*

Far more important, however, is the consideration of buying a bike that fits—and fits *now.* Remember how your folks bought you shoes that were a bit too big, so you wouldn't outgrow them so soon? The tendency to do the same with bikes is understandable, given the costs involved. But it's dangerous to put a kid on any bike that's too big; it's harder to control and to jump from in a crash.

To find a bike that fits, take your time, visit more than one shop, ask questions, pay attention to the answers, and test-ride a bunch of bikes. Bring a notebook with you to help keep things straight. Good luck.

The following words on frame construction, frame geometry, and gearing is information that isn't required for buying a bike but is very helpful in understanding terms and concepts. Skip this part if you're hankering to know the accessories you'll need for riding (chapter 2). You can always return to these pages when the roads and trails are pure ice

■ MORE ON FRAMES ■

Frame Construction

A quick tour of almost any good bike shop will provide examples of the two most common frame construction methods: TIG welding (the use of tungsten inert gas to weld together tubes—usually steel but sometimes aluminum—without employing lugs), and brass-brazing with lugs. (A lug is a short metal sleeve that accepts, surrounds, and joins two or more tubes. See photo c.) You'll find lugs more on road bikes than on mountain bikes, however, and they're waning in popularity even there. Too labor intensive.

If you're in a high-end shop, you might find frames that have been happily subjected to fillet brazing, a lovely but costly technique in which layer after layer of torch-melted brass solder is built up over each tube juncture. Such a shop might also have frames of welded or lugged titanium, welded metal matrix composites, lugged carbon fiber, or even "monocoque" one-piece carbon fiber—the frames with the most futuristic look of all.

Back in the realm of what most of us can hope to afford, however, are the welded and bonded aluminum frames. The welding process is similar to that used when TIG-welding steel tubes (often done with oversized tubes); "bonded" refers to the gluing of tubes into cast-aluminum lugs.

Have you got all that? Good. Now you can store it away. But keep this thought in mind: TIG-welding is open to view. Sloppy TIGing results in pinholes and gaps, which may or may not affect the frame down the road (or trail) but which doesn't give you confidence in the frame builder's techniques.

Frame Geometry

Look at the drawing and you'll see what forms the head-tube angle, bottom bracket height, chainstay length, and so on. That's the easy part. The trick is understanding how these numbers affect the ride. Frankly, it's a whole lot easier to *feel* it.

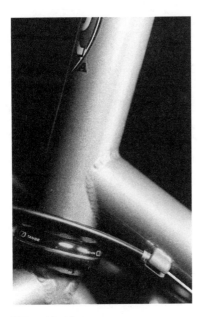

TIG welded frame

Fillet-brazed frame

Let's begin with bikes at either extreme. Racing bikes have extremely steep angles, while laid-back beach cruisers have more relaxed angles. The first provides you with fast turns and quick responses, the second with the kind of stable ride you'd enjoy for long, unhurried days in the saddle. Choose a head- and seat-tube angle roughly halfway between those extremes, it is thought, and most riders will be happy most of the time.

The industry standard at present is a head/seat measurement of 71/73. That's 71 and 73 degrees, a measurement of the angles you see described in the illustration and considerably steeper than were mountain bikes

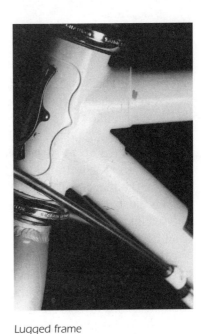

Lugged frame

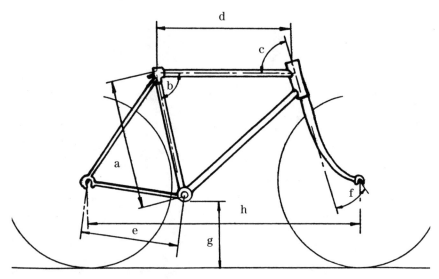

Frame Geometry

a) seat-tube length
b) seat-tube angle
c) head-tube length
d) top-tube length

e) chainstay length
f) fork rake
g) bottom bracket height
h) wheel base

when they first appeared. The numbers will make sense if you stare at the drawing and slowly increase and decrease the angles one at a time, imagining as you do so what effect it will have on wheel and rider placement. Soon you see that steeper angles will put the rider closer to the bars, in position more like a jockey who's eager to get around the track. Shallower angles, of course, do the opposite, tilting you back as if in an easy chair.

The concept of "fork rake" is most easily seen when you compare racing and touring thin-tire bikes. Notice the long, graceful, bump-smoothing angle on the touring bike's fork? And the nearly straight, precise-steering fork on the racing bike? Look again at two nonsuspension mountain bikes and you'll begin to see the difference between steep and sloping angles in head tubes, seat tubes, and forks.

Bottom brackets on mountain bikes are considerably higher than they are on touring bikes of identical size. The purpose should by now be obvious—to allow for ground clearance over obstacles and the ability to pedal without striking objects on the trail and in tight turns. And while head- and seat-tube angles in the past few years have gradually become steeper, bottom brackets have gotten higher, and wheelbases and chainstay lengths have shortened—all producing sportier, more trailworthy bikes. (Decreasing the length of chainstays brings the rear wheel up under the rider for better traction and tighter turns; this change, added to straighter forks and steeper angles elsewhere, produces shorter wheelbases.) And if sporty is what you want, you've got it waiting for you on the bike shop floor. You might have to look a little harder, however, for those that will be good for commuting and touring as well.

■ MORE ON GEARING ■

Many thin-tire-bike manufacturers publish literature on their cycles stating something like "33- to 101-gear range as equipped," or "100-inch gear high range." What is a 100-inch gear, and how is that number derived? It comes from this formula:

$$\frac{\text{\# teeth in front sprocket}}{\text{\# teeth in rear sprocket}} \times \text{wheel diameter in inches}$$

Take my touring bike, for example: The larger front sprocket has 54 teeth, the smallest back sprocket has 14.

$$\frac{54}{14} \times 27 = 104\text{-inch gear}$$

But this does *not* mean the bike will travel 104 inches down the road with one pump of the pedals. It refers instead to the number of inches in diameter the front wheel would be in a "direct-drive" setup, such as the old "high-wheelers" of the 1870s and 1880s. Those bikes had no complicated gearing, and therefore the single "gear" was determined by the size of the front wheel, to which the pedals were attached. Imagine a high-wheeler 104 inches in diameter, or more than 8½ feet high!

On the other end of the scale, the lowest gear on my thin-tire touring bike is 33.3 inches:

$$\frac{42}{34} \times 27 = 33.3$$

In this case the high-wheeler wouldn't be so high at all, and would look more like a child's tricycle. Now you can see the beauty of today's gearing, which allows you to race down mountains and to granny-gear your way to the top—*plus* have all the gear ratios between the extremes when you need them.

I know it's confusing. But you can make things far easier by looking closely at a bike. Imagine the chain affixed to the largest chain ring and the smallest freewheel cog (a combination producing the highest—hardest—gear). Let's assume the chain ring is three times the size of the rear cog. In this case, each time the pedals revolve once (that is, each time the chain ring is turned one time), the rear wheel will spin around three times. How far will that propel you down the road? That's easy, even without resorting to higher mathematics. Using a standard (thin-tire) 27-inch-diameter wheel, we merely multiply this diameter by pi (3.14) to obtain the circumference, then multiply again by three revolutions.

$$27'' \times 3.14 = 84.78'' \text{ (or about 7 feet for one revolution)}$$

$$7' \times 3 \text{ revolutions} = 21 \text{ feet}$$

Now imagine the chain on the smallest chain ring and the largest cog in the rear. Many triple cranksets have sprockets as small as and even smaller than the largest freewheel cog, but for our discussion we will imagine they are identical in size (possessing the same number of teeth). In this case (a one-to-one gear ratio), each time the rider pedals once, the rear wheel revolves only one time. And from the figures above we already know the bike would proceed only seven feet forward.

It stands to reason that moving seven feet with each pedal revolution would be far easier than propelling yourself twenty-one feet. When going uphill, therefore, and interested more in being able to continue pedaling than in covering distances quickly, we switch into our lower (easier) gears. When the summit is attained, or on the flat with the wind at our backs, the relative ease of pedaling and our gear options allow us to take advantage of the situation by switching into high (harder) gears. Think of hiking up a hill, when you take short steps, compared to your long, easy strides on level ground. The principle is the same.

Mountain bikes have 26-inch-diameter wheels instead of the thin-tire 27-inch standard, so make that adjustment when you do your calculations. Pay attention to your chain placement until you get the hang of how each gear feels. You'll soon find that the numbers are important guides when buying a bike or setting up a new chain ring/freewheel configuration, but that few riders ever think in terms of gear inches while in the saddle.

2

ACCESSORIES

If you thought you could put away your wallet after deciding upon and buying a bike, think again. Sure you've got the mount itself, a sleek beast capable of carrying you into (and out of) the wilds of city and trail. But what if it rains? Or you get a flat? And what if you want to pack a lunch and first-aid kit for trips into the backcountry, or pack your books for school or briefcase for the office? Which shoes are best for off-road travel? Which helmet should you wear? What's the best way to lock a bike, especially one with quick-release wheels and seatpost?

The primary purpose of this chapter is to inform you of the existence of the kinds of products available and the need for them, not to suggest one brand name over another, with a few exceptions. With this in mind, use the following to direct you to and help you assess both the older and the most recent offerings in the mountain bike world.

■ TOE CLIPS AND STRAPS/CLIPLESS PEDALS/PEDAL REFLECTORS ■

At first glance the use of clips and straps or clipless pedals on a mountain bike might appear suicidal. "What? Be clipped to a bike that's bouncing over curbs and boulders?!" The concern is understandable, but you'll learn very quickly that no matter what the terrain, your control (and therefore your safety) is greatly increased when your feet don't slip from the pedals. Newcomers to the sport will please notice that I did not say *are locked* to the pedals. Straps *can* be pulled tight, but are not by most fat-tire riders. And, in the event that gravity wins out over your bike-handling abilities, your feet will slip free almost automatically.

Of course, the tighter you pull the straps, to gain power on the pedal upstroke and to increase the feeling of being one with your bike, the greater the chance your feet won't slip free from the pedals in time before you hit the dirt. So too with the ever-more-popular clipless pedals. The more expensive of these models come equipped with maintenance-free sealed roller bearings and an adjustable tension to the snap-in locking mechanism. I strongly suggest that if you choose these, you start out with the pedals in the low-tension position—especially when taking them onto trails for the first time.

A number of companies offer beefy black plastic "mountain" clips that I've not been able to break, and "mountain" straps of woven nylon with a tensile strength sufficient to lift pianos. I thought at first these "mountain" products were just industry hype, until I learned while using them that not only are they of amazing industrial strength—needed with the thrashing they take—but that they're built a bit differently from thin-tire models as well. Some of the clips, for instance, have a wider mouth and a raised toe area to fit the larger shoes and boots and raised toe box of the footwear often worn by off-roaders. And the straps are a couple of inches longer for the same reason.

Pedal reflectors are advisable for those who will be single-tracking through the mountains and cycling dark country roads, and absolutely crucial for commuters (due to their great visibility resulting from the near-constant up and down movement).

▪ MIRROR ▪

For years I groused about the lousy, or at least unsatisfactory, mirrors available for mountain bikes and bikers. I found those tiny wrap-around-your-glasses mirrors to be too small, and didn't like resembling an insect with

CycleAware Reflex helmet-mounted mirror.

one antenna missing when removing my helmet and running into a store. The helmet-mounted and nicely engineered CycleAware Reflex has been an understandable hit with many riders, because the $1^5/_8$- $\times$ $1^1/_8$-inch mirror is large enough to view the world behind, attaches easily and yet can be removed and replaced again in seconds, stays in place no matter the terrain, and has a full 360-degree movement with built-in stops every 30 degrees. It also weighs almost nothing and can be tilted up out of view when you wish. Despite all these positive qualities, however, I could not accustom myself to holding my head still momentarily and glancing up to look back. Helmets get banged about when you take them off (and at times on narrow single-tracks, even while you have them on), and I found having to reposition the lens occasionally a bit of a pain. Many riders don't have these problems and like the fact that helmet-mounted mirrors weigh so little and keep one more item off the bike, so I'm probably the one out of sync.

What I wanted was a large-lens mirror at the handlebar, where I think a mirror belongs. But I didn't like the kind that attaches to the end of the bar, for it got knocked about or broken whenever laying my bike on its side. Nor did I like the style that affixes itself to the left-hand grip with a girth-increasing huge swath of Velcro, because it felt awkward in the hand and covered the far superior texture of the grip itself. Neither it nor the bar-end mirror could be placed completely out of the way. I tried every style mirror that appeared, but nothing was perfect.

And then, at last, a Mirrycle took place. Or, to be specific, a Mountain Mirrycle. The tiny Boulder, Colorado-based Mirrycle Corporation finally reengineered its universally loved thin-tire touring bike mirror for a mountain bike. Its large-diameter lens leaps into view when I glance toward it, and both the mirror arm and mirror itself revolve completely for infinite adjustment. It can be turned out of the way when on trails, and, like its thin-tire brother, it takes a licking without breaking. A water buffalo pulling a cart on a downtown Bombay street once rudely swung its huge head into my mirror as I attempted to pedal past it on the right. Its horn missed my forearm but whacked my Mirrycle, which swung nicely with the blow but remained coolly undisturbed. To my mind it's the perfect commuter's and tourer's mirror (no matter the country); it's even easy to install and comes with a list of replacement parts and prices. Don't buy any mirror for your mountain bike until you've seen this one. And if your neighborhood bike shop doesn't carry it, whisper the words that are rarely uttered inside shops—"mail order" (which is how I had to buy mine). That might stir them into action.

■ WATER-BOTTLE CAGES/WATER BOTTLES/ HYDRATION SYSTEMS ■

I was among the first to scoff at mountain cages, those bottle holders trumpeted to withstand the abuse of tough trails. But after several years of seeing what happens to regular thin-tire cages when stressed in ways for which they were clearly not designed (that is, trail bashing), especially when holding the large-capacity water bottles, I bow my head to the engineers.

Water bottles too have undergone a transformation. Buy the cheap ones and they'll crush when you push the lid down tight. Better bottles are formed of denser plastic walls, to withstand rough treatment. And you'll thank yourself later if you go to the trouble now of finding bottles that won't leak when lying on their sides.

Larger bottles hold twenty-eight ounces (just four shy of a quart); the smaller hold twenty. So how many bottles do you need on a ride? Well, a human working hard in 90-degree heat needs ten quarts (that's $2\frac{1}{2}$ gallons) of water replenishment every day. And while riding trails is tremendous fun, your body still interprets it as hard work. Remember to drink before you're thirsty: Your body actually becomes slightly dehydrated before you feel dry.

I pack along two large water bottles for most one-day trail rides, though I have mounted as many as eight for extended desert trips. With water weighing in at eight pounds per gallon, you'll of course not want to pack any more than necessary, but be sure you have the bottles and containers you'll need to fill when you start planning extended backcountry rides as well as a water purification system if you're going to be away from reliable water sources for any amount of time. (See chapter 5 for notes on the waterborne disease you want only to *read* about—giardia—and the almost weightless water purification tablets that will keep it at bay.)

And then there's that other storage device, the water-tank-on-your-back portable hydration system called, appropriately, CamelBak. When first hearing about this invention I was reminded of the time on my world ride in '74 when my buddy and I parked our bikes at the pyramids and rode two rented camels into the desert—though we were *sitting* upon our hump's worth of water. When I first saw a CamelBak I was in fact in the desert of southern Arizona. A mountain biker was pedaling toward me with what from a distance resembled a tiny garter snake at his chin. As he neared I saw this was a plastic tube designed for hands-free sipping, and when he

CAMELBAK in Narrow
Gauge pack

The Packster

Camelbak with Integrator Utility belt

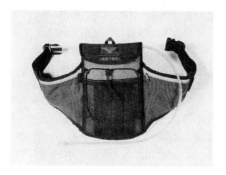

The Go-Be

passed I could see it emanated from a black polyurethane bag that clung to his back like a baby koala bear. Neat.

Now, of course, there are in addition to the original seventy-ounce leak-proof packs both larger and smaller models, plus ThermoBaks and IceBaks (think of thermoses and ice packs), waist-pack models (with longer garter-snake hoses), and light-weight backpacks in which the water bag sits—plus everything else you'd normally carry somewhere else on your bike.

And here's where things get tricky. The biker/inventors out there suddenly saw the opportunity to offer mountain bikers a chance to save the weight of a rear rack (to support panniers and top-of-the-rack bags) and water-bottle cages, plus the advantage

CAMELBAK Unibottle System

of not having to worry about what they'd left on their bikes when locking them up in the city or at a trailhead. It took about a minute for a half dozen different designs of CamelBak-toting backpacks to pop up.

Some of these packs, like the one offered by CamelBak itself, offer regular backpacklike pockets into which you can dump all your gear. Others, like the Forest Hump* I've been riding with for months, have an interesting modular design in which there's a compartment ready-made for all those things mountain bikers deem essential—tools, a mini–air pump, spare tube, even an energy bar pocket on the strap so it's accessible while you're riding (!), plus several small pockets in which you can store remaining items (keys, wallet, trail or city map, Band-Aids, snakebite kit . . .) in a tight-against-you fashion so they won't jangle about while you're hopping curbs and buses and water bars. In addition, there's a waist-belt accessory that has clip-on receptacles for the addition of a 240-cubic-inch (the volume, roughly, of an extra-large sweatshirt) cargo pocket. And because the 500-denier** Cordura- (heavy-duty packcloth) enclosed CamelBak is between you and all your gear, nothing pokes you while you ride.

Don't buy the first pack you see. Chances are your bike shop will carry only one model, and in the excitement to get started you might purchase something you won't like best later on. Just as with a bike, do the research.

▪ TIRES ▪

Four quick points: First, buy skinwalls—not the heavy, dead-feeling gum rubber; second, while wide, low-pressure, full-knobby tires provide the best for fast urban commutes and touring exclusively will want high-pressure,

---

* The Forest Hump pack is put out by CycoActive Products of Seattle. I have added their address and toll-free number to the appendix, only because you probably won't find this product or their ingenious BarMap map holder and BarMap OTG map holder/handlebar bag in your local shop.

** *Denier* is defined as "a number indicating the weight in grams of 9,000 meters of the thread used to weave the fabric." And the *ounce* number ascribed to a fabric is the weight of one square yard of that fabric. Really, all you need to know is that these terms provide the information we need on *relative* thicknesses—and therefore, in many cases, the durability—of fabric. The greater the number, the thicker and and possibly stronger the material.

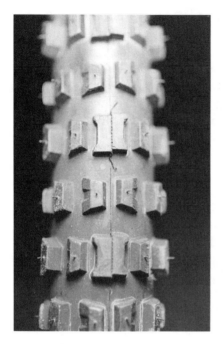 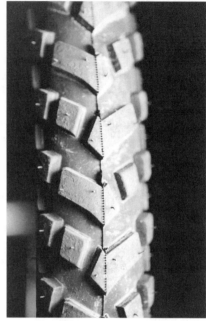

Specialized Hardpack tire   Tioga Farmer John tire

fast-rolling skins; fourth, while there are some lovely tires that give you a bit of both worlds (trail and pavement), don't expect them to provide the *best* of both worlds.

Many mountain bike tires are now so specialized that they require you to orient the tire for direction when installing it on your rim. In addition, some designs are made only for use on the front wheel, others for the rear, while some are known to offer best cornering or climbing or even best braking power in the wet. Most are now of a wide-ranging variable pressure that allows you to fine-tune your traction to dirt road and trail conditions, and those featuring an interlocking center bead (like the Specialized Cross Roads II) can be pumped hard (80 psi) for pavement and hard-packed dirt road travel, or ridden soft (35–40 psi) in loose dirt and sand.

As discussed in chapter 1, commuters often choose the puncture-resistant tires beaded with Kevlar (the material used in many law-enforcement protective vests); trail riders who want to protect against cactus thorns also use these tires, or add the hard plastic tire liners (Mr. Tuffy is one popular brand) or make use of the liquid Slime that plugs a hole (up to ³/₁₆ inch in size) in your tube as soon as it appears. And while commuters usually opt for the thinnest and highest-pressure tires around (like the Specialized Fat Boy at 1.25 inches wide and 100 psi, or Performance Fast City at 1.25 inches wide and a variable pressure of 45–90 psi), some ride with one of my favorites—the internal-tread design (grooved) Avocet Cross (40–90 psi and available in 1.25 inches, 1.5 inches, and 1.9 inches). The 1.5-inch Avocet Cross is an excellent all-around tire for dirt roads, jeep trails, very easy single- and double-tracking, commuting, and touring. It isn't as fast on pavement as its thinner brother, of course, nor does it give the traction of an external-tread wider tire. Even the 1.9-inch Avocet Cross loses out, in my opinion, to the external-tread 1.9-inch Specialized Cross Roads II in terms of traction in loose dirt and rock, but it's much faster on pavement.

A special note for winter riders: Almost any wide knobby will do well in snow that isn't up to the axles, but when it's packed down and turned to ice you'll need more than rubber to remain upright. You'll need to chain up! Some shops, and almost any mail-order catalog, offer chains that guarantee you a better chance of staying up on ice.

A final suggestion is that you think also in terms of a tire's *height*. Because narrow tires are shorter in sidewall height than are wide tires, the distance between the rim and whatever you're encountering on the road or trail is decreased—perhaps critically. It's critical, that is, if you're riding with little air pressure, for there's always the chance to pinch your tube (the infamous snakebite double puncture) or, worse, put a blip in your rim.

■ BIKE SECURITY ■

It's inevitable, unfortunately, that someday, somewhere, some lowlife is going to see your bike and think about ripping it off. What is *not* inevitable is the thief's success.

So how to go about protecting your investment? First, be smart about where you leave it. Try to think like a criminal: If you were stealing your bike, would you prefer it locked to a post in full view of the people inside the coffee shop, or secured to the fence behind the place? Best of all for the thief, of course, would be if someone were dumb enough to leave the bike unlocked "just for a minute" while popping inside for a cup.

The next thing to think about is what type of lock to buy. For a while a good strong U-lock was sufficient insurance. Now you have to keep the creeps from getting enough leverage between the lock to pry it apart, something that can be done by adding Vetta Bad Bones (steel bars) to it, or adding a second kind of lock (this with the probably too-hopeful notion that a thief will be packing *either* what's necessary to pry open a U-lock *or* what he needs to cut a cable), or using one of the new designs made to repel attempts at prying, cutting, and breaking (like the Ultra Bike Club lock I now use to secure my bike in the big city. It's put out by the same folks who build The Club for cars).

Rhode Gear Citadel XL shows the advantage of a long shackle.

And then there's the problem of keeping people from stealing your quick-release front wheel and seatpost/saddle, and anything else that's quickly removable. Long-shackle U-locks are good to keep the front wheel in place (never, never think you're locking your bike by securing only the front wheel to a post), but if you're using only one you'll need to lock both the wheel and the frame to something that's very secure. This does not include trees with trunks the size of your top tube; they can be sawed through in seconds. Vetta had produced a triangular Verdict Lock that both prohibits prying and fits the wheel/frame/post distance requirement. If your U-lock is a short-shackle model (that is, not long enough to engage the front wheel), use it to secure your frame and buy a lightweight cable lock to secure the front wheel. Granted, such a cable could be cut through quickly with large bolt cutters, but a thief might not be so ready to risk detection to steal just a wheel.

My own solution is to pack *two* large locks when I'm commuting. I use the Ultra Bike Club to secure the frame to a post or parking meter (making sure that the bike and lock cannot be simply lifted free of the meter), and a short-shackle U-lock to secure the wheel to the frame. (There's an Ultra Bike Club Junior as well, a smaller model perfect for this second task. But I already had a smaller U-lock and didn't want to buy another.) It takes me only seconds longer to feel confident, but you're probably shaking your head at the thought of all that weight—a bit over five pounds. Well, yes, you wouldn't want to pack such tonnage when racing along trails. But when commuting, it simply ensures a good workout.

Carrying these locks, however, can be a pain. I always commute with one or two panniers (saddlebags), and so just toss them into one of the compartments. Some riders hang them from their saddle rails, or from a small U-lock holder that clamps around the seatpost, or bungee them to the top of their rear racks. But most carry them in the U-lock clamps designed by the individual lock companies for attachment directly to the frame. Pay attention to these clamps when choosing a lock; some are far more secure than others. If you're like me, you want a bike that's silent beneath you, not clanking about when you go over bumps. For those of you with smaller frames, see how much room you have inside your main triangle (the triangle formed by the seat, top, and down tubes) before deciding where to pack your lock or mount a second bottle cage. A single water bottle, after all, should be sufficient for most commutes. (Though a second—filled with ammonia—is a great defense against dogs.)

Some commuters prefer to discourage thieves by making the chore of theft just too much trouble. Yes, tying a Doberman to your frame would do the trick. But most of these riders choose to make their point with huge, case-hardened tempered-steel link chains, secured by equally menacing case-hardened locks or a small but hefty-looking U-lock like Kryptonite's EV Disc Lock. Kryptonite sells this lock along with its massive nylon-webbed New York Chain in both three- and six-foot lengths. Packing weighty steel link chains is a pain, of course, but will probably succeed in convincing a thief to have a go at a lock more his size.

Thus far you've protected your frame and front wheel; the quick-release rear wheel is seldom stolen by itself because of the difficulty in removing it—especially when the frame, or frame and front wheel, is locked securely. But this still leaves your expensive-to-replace seatpost and saddle at risk. Watch some commuters lock up for the day in big cities and you'll see them flip the q-r lever and pack the seatpost and saddle with them. Even if they're fortunate enough not to get seatpost grease on their clothing, if they fail to plug their open seat tube with a cork (or, preferably, a black rubber stopper), they're leaving it exposed to rain and dust. This debris will foul the tube, and the bottom bracket, too, if it's not sealed inside.

There is the option of replacing the q-r skewer with a two-inch-long, 6-millimeter bolt, double nutted on one end to discourage even further the thief who thinks he won't be noticed while working away with a couple of spanners. If you're a trail rider as well, however, and like to raise and lower your saddle for steep climbs and descents, this isn't going to work.

Two products offer an alternative. The currently available Seat Locker, distributed by Avenir and available in most well-stocked bike shops, is modeled after "The Seat Leash" (no longer made) that I purchased long ago and still use. It is a black, PVC-coated, $^3/_{32}$-inch galvanized aircraft cable that loops around the saddle rails on one end and the seatstay at the other. Granted, a small pair of wire cutters can quickly make it history. But then it's often too conspicuous for a criminal to have at a seatpost with a tool.

The second product is one I've not yet tried. It's similar in concept to the Seat Leash, but has the advantage of running *inside* your seat tube and is therefore invisible. The inexpensive Postmaster weighs only twenty-four grams, and is secured in the frame below a bottle-cage bolt. If your shop doesn't carry it, call the manufacturer—Innovations in Cycling (see the appendix for all addresses and phone numbers).

▪ AIR PUMP ▪

Hand pumping has never been among my favorite pastimes, and filling a huge ATB tire makes the act even less appealing. But it still beats walking. Larger-volume pumps are available to cut down the time you'll spend flailing away, but most popular are the tiny models that fit easily into a fanny pack or pannier. If things continue at this pace, next year's model will fit behind your ear. Be sure your pump is securely mounted if you're affixing it to your frame, and for heaven's sake don't leave it there when you leave your bike. Pump theft, you know. If you're real lazy, or in a hurry, try the compressed-gas cartridge inflator kits. But you'll pay a hefty price for the convenience.

■ FENDERS ■

I'll have more to say on these in chapter 4 , but for now you should know that they are available in various lengths and widths. And they now vary widely in

Pumping up a tire.

attachment—a real boon to weekday commuters who go crazy on the trails come Saturday and don't want to hassle with fenders in the dirt. For the past year, however, I've used two absolutely no-hassle fenders to keep both road and trail spray off me, and love the results. Both the Mudslide (front mudguard) and Backscratcher (rear splash guard) are put out by Headland Bicycle Accessories. The widest and longest wraps will of course do the most complete job in protecting you from the elements, and are a must if you commute in your work duds. (I strongly suggest the use of thread-locking compound on your permanently mounted full-on fenders to keep them steady.)

I should also add a note on CycoActive's splash guard called the Fender Rollup. This

Headland Bicycle Accesories "The Mudslide" front mud guard.

THE NEW COMPLETE MOUNTAIN BIKER

Headland Bicycle Accessories "Backscratcher" rear splash guard.

novel item is five inches by ten inches when attached to the down tube, yet rolls up and stores inside a seat pack!

■ RACKS ■

There have been light-years of improvements in this department since my first cross-country ride in '65. Back then we used heavy racks with movable support arms and a spring-loaded top. They connected to the seatstays with metal clamps, and on my world ride in '74 the weight we carried made them fall again and again toward the center-pull brakes (until we thought to add tiny hose clamps to the stays). The racks swayed in the breeze and threatened to crack. But those were the old days. I test a lot of products, receive a number of readers' letters, talk with bike magazine editors and bike shop workers often—and I haven't heard of *any* presently offered racks breaking on the road or trail.

But that doesn't mean they're all the same. Starting at the top (in both quality and cost) are the Bruce Gordon racks, the chro-moly, hand-brazed, baked-on, black-epoxy-finish frame extensions that look like pieces of sculpture and ride like they were born on your bike. Next comes Blackburn, made of lifetime-warranty, heavy-duty aluminum, with special support designs for mountain bikes. And after these industry leaders come a host of look-alikes like Rhode Gear and the mail-order company Performance Bicycle. Buy carefully, and when putting any rack on your bike, perform the operation with care (and a little thread-locking compound). The abuse these things take, and the strain under which they fulfill their purpose in life, is enormous.

If you pack a lot of weight, you should consider both front and rear racks. Most front racks are the same height as rear racks, but there are those that ride lower. Think long and hard before you put front-wheel low-riders on your mountain bike. I've had to test these systems for a couple of companies and found it extremely unpleasant: Fall into a deep rut and you'll end up knocking off your front panniers; try to wind through brush, cactus, or high rocks and you'll bang up your bags. To my mind, front low-riders on ATBs just don't make any sense, as the shorter, wider wheels and tires of mountain bikes, and their larger frames, make them so stable that the slight amount of stability gained by the lowered center of gravity fails to offset the problems incurred. And, a difficulty almost as great for those

Headland Bicycle Accessories "Utility X" rear carrier.

tourers who need every space possible to carry their gear, there's no level rack top on front-wheel low-rider racks.

Many mountain bike frames these days are so souped up for high performance on the trails that mounting a rack in back, much less in front, is a near impossibility. Headland Bicycle Accessories has come, again, to the rescue. Its novel Utility-X Rack bolts not to the frame but to the seatpost, is made of aircraft-grade aluminum, and has a forty-pound weight limit. You can't hang panniers from it, but it's large enough to handle the largest top-of-the-rack bags. Or a gross of energy bars.

▪ LIGHTS ▪

This was once a subject exclusively for commuters, but more and more mountain bikers are choosing to pedal trails after dark.

Let's start with something I talked about earlier: pedal reflectors. Be sure you've got these on both pedals. Add a flashing VistaLite or Cateye to your seat or rear rack, and the only car that will hit you from behind is one that's aiming for you. (Flashing lights are amazingly economical: They cost little, do a lot, and run for up to five hundred hours on a couple of double A's.)

If your two-wheeled travels don't keep you out after dark on a regular basis, you might be happy with the krypton- or halogen-bulb headlights that affix to a small plastic mount on your handlebars. These slip easily into place when pulled from your pannier, and operate on two or four double A's and so are not all that heavy. Don't expect them to light up the road ahead like an automobile headlight, or even as well as the lights discussed below, but for low cost and weight and great convenience they can't be beat. Some of these tiny models even offer rechargeable battery packs.

And now we come to the *real* lighting systems, the handlebar- or helmet-mounted lights that will make cars think you're a motorcycle, and will freeze deer in their tracks. These things are state-of-the-art and are priced accordingly, so before you buy I suggest you flip through the last six months' supply of bike magazines and find a review of the latest models. Most offer rechargeable NiCad battery packs that hang from your belt or rest inside a water-bottle cage, and some models give you the choice of mounting the light (or even dual-beam lights) on the handlebar *or* helmet. Which is preferable? Well, that depends. The largest handlebar-mounted system might be best for urban commuting and open-country, after-dark dirt-road and trail riding. But the helmet-mount is best for twisty single-tracking and for illuminating something that isn't directly in front of your bike.

For those of you who will complain about the cost of these systems, and the fact that their light fades to black after three to six hours of burn time, think for a moment what bike lights were in very recent yesteryears. You don't have to be a graybeard to recall the popular flashlight holders (made of steel, by the way) we used to clamp to our handlebars. Or the generator systems whose tiny metal wheels ran along the tire side-

Commuter utilizes handlebar-mounted headlamp.

wall to produce a wavering beam of illumination—until we stopped at an intersection and the world went black. The rear generators that required us to run wire clear to the handlebars for the headlight blessedly have been replaced by the one-piece, fork-mounted generator headlight.

There was a problem in this design, however, as anyone who has ever gotten anything stuck in a moving front wheel will instantly surmise. The rider was warned to keep the generator fixing clamp fixed *tightly* to the fork. Something less obvious, however, was what could happen if, while coasting carefully

Marwi USA handlebar-mounted bike light.

and reaching over the handlebar to flip the lever that engaged the generator, a thumb slipped. I never thought about it until I read a first-person account of a fellow bike commuter who had done just what he and I and a thousand other dopes too much in a hurry to stop when flipping our generators against the front tire sidewall had done for years. His thumb squeaked off the wet lever (it was raining lightly, he wrote) and into the turning spokes. In the blink of an eye he was peeled from the saddle to the pavement before his front wheel, whereupon his own bike ran over him. He was lucky to escape with only a broken thumb and a few bent spokes.

■ CYCLOMETERS ■

These aren't a necessity, but sometimes it's nice to know *exactly* how far it is to work, how quickly you've ridden a trail, how fast you're traveling during a workout. They are very light and relatively easy to install; your main difficulty lies in choosing which of the zillion models you want. I suggest one that shows two readouts always. Mine is set up to show current speed and trip distance always, and when I get back home or return to the trail-head I hit the button that provides total time elapsed, average speed, and fastest speed attained. Cadence and clock features are also present on most bike computers.

There is a very real danger to these entertaining and fascinating gadgets, however, and I very nearly became statistical proof of this on my initial cyclometer-rigged ride. It's impossible to look at and play with your cyclometer and watch the road at the same time, as I learned when I missed a parked car by inches.

■ CLOTHING ■

I'll provide specific suggestions for particular riding styles in following chapters, but for now here are a few general comments that may be of some assistance when starting off.

Riding Gloves

Ride hard all day on thin tires and the pressure against tiny nerves in the heels of your hands will make the two smallest fingers on each hand feel numb. Beat the trails on a mountain bike for half that long and your fingers will be both numb and sore, the latter from constant vibrations and occasional hard jolts. Any cycling gloves will do, though a few brands have a bit too much padding for my taste; especially on a mountain bike you must be protected from the bar, yet at the same time you must have a very firm grip on it. Test the various thicknesses and fabrics until you find one that's right for you. And don't forget the importance of *good* grips when it comes to hand comfort on a bike.

Shorts

Almost every mountain biker I encounter these days is in a pair of Lycra shorts with chamois or other inserts for comfort. I didn't ride in these myself until more and more of my workout and trail rides began to take place in the humid Midwest; my long-preferred Patagonia Stand-Up and Sportif USA hiking shorts and JCPenney undershorts were soaked in sweat in twenty minutes and stayed wet for hours. Now I don a pair of Patagonia Baggies over the top of my Lycras, and I've got comfort *and* pockets.

Every year another manufacturer puts out a new line of mountain biker shorts. These have chamois or padded inserts, and look like lightweight hiking shorts. But almost all have cargo pockets, the openings of which sit low on the leg. They are not very deep, and because of this and their location— not in front or back but exactly on the side of the thigh—the contents spill out whenever you sit down. One model I tested had a Velcro closing along the top, but even then the contents felt awkward, hanging as they do when you're in the saddle.

Shoes

Visit a well-stocked bike shop and you'll find an amazing selection of footwear designed specifically for off-road riding. Don't make a hasty decision—the right cycling shoes are critical for comfortable and effective pedaling. Most shoes resemble somewhat rugged touring shoes, and offer recessed clipless pedal attachment panels so they won't be in the way when you're not on the bike. Many riders, myself included, prefer instead to ride with toe clips and straps and low-cut (shoe-height) hiking boots that meet the following requirements:

1. a very stiff midsole, to reduce pedal strain on the instep muscles as well as to increase pedal efficiency;
2. a tread that is sufficiently aggressive to allow for good traction when pushing the bike, yet not so ribbed or corrugated that it causes great difficulty getting into and out of the clips;

3. a wide, stiff toe box that will not compress after hours of pressure against the clips (thereby causing toe pain); and

4. all-day comfort both in and out of the saddle.

Everyone has his or her own favorite. My shoe of choice is heavy Vasque Clarion Impact Low. Of all the boots I've ever tested in the saddle, these are by far the stiffest, and are thus my preference when pushing the heaviest loads or tackling the toughest trails. (By the way, a quick in-store test of stiffness is to hold the shoe by its toe and heel, then attempt to bend it *downward,* in the opposite direction as you would when walking or hiking. This is the way a shoe will flex when pushing pedals and you want as little flexibility in this direction as possible.)

A new product coming to the market is a platform pedal similar to those used by triathletes. It's a stiff platform and toe clip that enables you to wear any type of shoe. It will have a guarded toe-piece, and a couple of angled straps that can be pulled tight or left somewhat loose. The platforms will weigh 5½ ounces each, and best of all you can wear any shoe you wish, no matter its flex. (The address of the company that makes it, VO2 MAX, Inc., is in the appendix.)

Eyewear

Glasses are a good idea whenever you're in the saddle. Catch a single junebug in the eye or strain your eyes through long days of sunny skies, and you'll know the importance of having a shield of glass or plastic between you and the world—especially when traveling at good speed along a trail. Twigs, tree limbs, dust, rocks kicked up from a fellow biker's rear knobby all can take their toll. Sunglasses are, understandably, a hot seller to mountain bikers, as a glance at any mail-order bike catalog will prove.

Unfortunately, for those of us who spend many hours pedaling roads and trails, buying the wrong pair of glasses can be downright dangerous. Almost any pair of shades will give your eyes some relief from the glare of sunlight. But not all will protect them from the ultraviolet (UV) rays that can cause damage. And because any darkened lens causes our pupils to dilate, if the sunglasses don't screen out UV rays they are actually *more* dangerous than no glasses at all in this regard. So read the labels on sunglasses, and don't buy anything that doesn't come guaranteed to have UV protection.

Riding at the edge at southern Utah's Moqui Dugway.

High mountain riding near
Telluride, Colorado.

An early-morning ride past
Kentucky cornfields.

Catching a ride to the top at Vermont's Killington Ski Resort.

Home for the night after riding the trails in Ketchum and Sun Valley, Idaho.

Mountain bikers explore the past in Wyoming's Teton Valley.

Two bikers compare mounts near the town of Guilin, China.

Pedaling past sandstone hills at Capitol Reef National Park, Utah.

FBI Agent Dana Ward enjoys a blue-sky day off work in Arizona's Saguaro National Monument.

Lupines taller than her mountain bike surround this trail rider in Nova Scotia.

Winter wonderland at Utah's Bryce Canyon National Park.

Break time on the jungle-like Lost Valley
Bike Trail west of St. Louis, Missouri.

Fully loaded mountain biker on
St. Mary's Glacier Loop in Colorado.

Hawk's Bill Crag in northern Arkansas. This rider hid her bike in the
woods when she reached the Upper Buffalo Wilderness boundary
(bikes aren't allowed in wilderness areas), then hiked a couple of miles to
spend the night at one of the best campsites in all the Midwest.

Dr. James Sheedy, a clinical professor at the University of California at Berkeley and chairman of the National Society to Prevent Blindness, provides the following basic guidelines to keep in mind when shopping:

1. Make sure they block 99–100 percent of *both* UV-A and UV-B radiation, because there is clear medical evidence to show that lifetime UV exposure bears a significant relationship to cataract development. Be sure the label says this plainly, for some manufacturers will state "100 Percent UV Protection," which really means that the glasses meet 100 percent of American National Standards Institute's (ANSI) currently lower requirements.

2. Sunglasses should fit close to the face. A great deal of light can pour into the eyes if they don't. Larger lenses will of course block more UV rays, as will wraparound styles or those with sideshields.

3. Pick the darkness of the lens that provides the greatest comfort to the eyes in the conditions you'll be wearing them. This "light absorption" percentage (present on some sunglass labels) is a matter of personal taste, not a medical requirement.

4. Avoid lenses of very saturated or bright colors. They can make it difficult to read traffic lights properly.

Sunglasses are now a billion-dollar industry in America. Competition for this huge market and consumers' increased awareness of the need for adequate eyewear mean that today you can sometimes find glasses with the necessary UV-ray protection—and even the proper labeling telling you this—in drug- and department stores.

But what of the overall durability of the "cheap" shades? Dr. Howard Donner, an emergency room physician in Telluride and a faculty member of the Wilderness Medical Society warns in his "Solar Radiation and the Wilderness Eye" presentations that the acrylic plastic used in many such lenses scratches easily, can shatter into dangerous shards, can actually melt if left on a hot dashboard, and may give some people headaches due to poor visual sharpness. It's better to pay a bit more for the CR 39 higher-grade plastic, and best of all to choose polycarbonate (unbreakable) sunglasses, with a protective antiscratch coating, for high-impact activities.

For those of you who'll be pedaling high mountain trails, protective eyewear is even more critical, because ultraviolet radiation increases 4 percent with every thousand feet of elevation. No matter how high or low your trail, however, you can cut the UV rays reaching your sunglasses by the simple trick of adding a visor to your helmet. I've done this through the add-on Bell Helmet visors (removable and reattachable), and the considerably longer neoprene Duckbill visor that slips over any helmet. It's offered by the California manufacturer Better Visions, whose address is in the appendix.

A smart, well-equipped cyclist—providing she's wearing sun screen.

Remember that eyes require protection when they're outside for many hours even on cloudy days, when between 60 and 80 percent of UV rays still reach the earth. And, if you're one of the 135 million Americans wearing prescription glasses, you have the choice of relatively inexpensive clip-on shades; large, unfortunately boxy-looking plastic glasses that fit over your prescription glasses (I find these just too cumbersome, especially when worn with a helmet and headband); and the far more expensive but smaller pop-in prescription inserts that some sunglass makers fit behind the shades.

Finally, make sure you buy sunglasses that will stay on your head while you're bouncing along the trail. A pair of Chums or other cotton eye retainers will help with this, and also let your specs hang from around your neck while you're busy consulting a map and compass to see where in the world you are. (For information on goggles, see chapter 4.)

Helmets

I won't bother to repeat the statistics you see each year in bike magazines and newspapers. Suffice it to say that no helmet is as comfortable as wearing no helmet at all, but any lid beats the consequences of a serious head injury.

Make sure your helmet fits snugly but is comfortable, and meets either the ANSI Z90.4 or Snell Memorial Foundation standards; the helmet or box will be labeled accordingly. Then wear it properly, which means not cocked back on your head like a bonnet, which exposes your forehead to a world of possible knocks, but flat on your noggin (look in the mirror) only a couple of fingers' width above the eyebrows. You should be able to see the lip of the helmet when you look up.

■ BIKE BAGS ■

The bags you'll want will depend on what type of riding you'll be doing, whether commuting, touring, or taking day trips, etc. Here is a general overview of the many different kinds of bags available.

On-Person

Fanny packs are far more popular with mountain bikers than with thin-tire cyclists, perhaps because so many fat-tire enthusiasts prefer to keep their bikes "clean"—that is, free of the heavy racks and packs that tend to impair fast trail riding. Another reason is cost, for even the nicest fanny packs—and there are dozens from which to choose, including some wonderfully designed beauties that become part of a backpack put out by the same manufacturer—cost less than a rack and panniers combined.

Cyclist with fanny pack.

If money is no problem and you need more storage space, consider one of the high-tech backpacks made with mountain bikers and day hikers in mind. But be sure it works well for both. Try it on in the store and keep it on while you ask yourself if the straps and waist belt are so large that they would bother you during trail rides. If the answer is no, ask yourself if they are large enough to make day hiking comfortable when packed with gear. If you can't be sure until you've pedaled with it, tell the store owner you must be able to bring it back within a week if it doesn't pan out. If the answer is no, mail-order it. You'll have to eat the postage, but at least your return privilege is intact.

Wider than either a fanny pack or a biker-backpack is the "bicycle messenger bag," which hangs across one shoulder and usually has (they always *should* have) a wide but thin waist belt attached to keep it from flapping in

Commuting bags come in handy.

the breeze. The one I have is a Cycle Sac designed by former New York bike messenger Paul Rosenfield. It is made of waterproofed Cordura, and is of a size sufficient for small art portfolios. Perfect for the college crowd, it also lets the rest of us remain on two wheels even when the load for the office is large. (I've tried without success to determine if Paul is still making his Cycle Sacs. Performance Bicycle mail-order catalog now offers a bag of similar design, however, as does the company making McEnroe Brothers Courier Bags.)

Rack Packs/Duffels

There are scores of rear-wheel, rack-top bags to choose from. They differ in obvious ways—material (most often in the weight of Cordura), overall size, number of pockets, and cost, but most important is something far less noticeable to the eye: method of attachment. If you're thinking of this becoming your everyday commuting bag, imagine how it will be to attach and remove the pack every time you board up and leave your bike.

Some of the largest duffels, by the way, have special compartments for your U-lock, shoes, helmet, water bottle, and minipump.

Panniers

So many choices! I've tested dozens over the years, and if I carried less gear I would find a number of them to be adequate. I ride with bags made by several different companies while on trails and crosstown errands, but when I must pack my heaviest winter loads on tour, and any other time when I need space and great accessibility, there's only one system—Robert Beckman Designs. Built to custom fit the amazingly strong Bruce Gordon racks, I can pile in half my earthly belongings, leave on a multistate backcountry jeep trail and dirt road tour, and never give a moment's thought to rack or pack problems. Bob Beckman's bags, by the way, which were originally called Needle Works, are made to fit Blackburn-style racks as well. (Address in the appendix.)

A fully loaded bike as trusty steed

Almost any bike magazine will contain a number of pannier company advertisements. Send a postcard requesting a catalog and price sheet, visit the bike shops to see which brands they carry, and begin your search in earnest. Remember the advice given above: If you're considering a pannier as your always-present-around-town-and-on-trail bag, pay particular attention to the ease of mounting and detachment. And be sure to buy a pannier cover (rain cover) before you need it. The heavy Cordura most bags are made of takes a long time to dry.

Briefcases

Several companies make stylish Cordura bike briefcases that mount secure-ly to a rack, and hide the mounting hardware (usually a spring-tension strap and hooks) nicely behind a zipper or Velcro flap. Most are too much like briefcases in size to admit all the other necessities that are normally carried in a biker's "possibles bag"—poncho, tools, pump. . . . A good com-muting system would be a small pannier on one side of the rear rack, your briefcase on the other. Once at work you can dump the pannier at your desk and take the briefcase to meetings.

And then there's the somewhat nerdy-looking option of simply tossing your briefcase into a shopping basket–style pannier. This convenient pack can be fixed somewhat permanently (with small hose clamps) to your rear rack, so you won't have to worry about disengaging it when you get to work. (On second thought, who would want to steal one?) They're sized to accept a full paper grocery store sack on each side, and are in my mind a better way to carry a backpack full of books than on your back—especially in sum-mer. When not in use the sides and bottom collapse, fold up, and can be snapped closed.

The chance of a pedestrian reaching into your basket pannier and lift-ing out your briefcase while you're leaning forward looking for a break in the traffic is probably very small. But if I packed a briefcase in this manner, I would secure the handle to the basket with a bungee, just in case.

Seat Bags

Under-the-saddle bags for mountain bikes now range from hamster-sized Cordura sacks barely large enough for a tube and multipurpose tool, to huge wedge-shaped bags that blossom from beneath your derriere like the mouth of an old-time Victrola. I don't use these bags when commuting or during my workout or near-the-house trail rides, because I pack everything I need in a single pannier and can't see any sense in having to remove a second bag each time I pop into a store or stop for a cup of coffee. I've yet to see a seat pack large enough to carry a lot of gear securely *and* disengage from the bike fast enough not to be a pain, so I end up using one only on long back-country tours—when there's so much other stuff on the bike that I'm always near it anyway and needn't worry about removing troublesome bags.

Handlebar Bags

A number of companies produce bags that offer a small amount of storage space, and a very small viewing area of the city or trail map you might be using. By far my favorites, however, are two items offered by Seattle's CycoActive Products—the BarMap and BarMap OTG. Both are great when following trails you don't know by heart. They're built to hold the maps in a convenient place and out of the rain. Best of all, they offer the kind of *large* viewing area

The BarMap is an ingenious map holder and bag.

that I require to figure out which turn it was that I missed.

The BarMap is a map holder only, which lets you see the map on one side, the route directions on the other, while the BarMap OTG is an ingenious map holder and bag that provides an 8½- by 11-inch clear vinyl pocket on Cordura backing, yet folds up to a space-saving 5 inches by 6 inches. In that form a second clear pocket is in view (this can hold trail-

following notes or another map), and two additional pockets hold energy bars, a compass, etc. Both bags attach easily to the stem; the BarMap OTG closes securely with Velcro and has nylon borders that I've yet to rip or perforate—even with all the hammering I've given them in seasons of hard trail use.

Tom Myers, the designer of the BarMap, suggests that you copy the map and trail-following directions and leave the book or original topographic or Forest Service map behind. Any vinyl will pick up some of the ink from photocopies if they're left in place for days, so don't. Treating the vinyl with Armor All will also reduce this problem.

▪ FIRST AID ▪

There are a couple of ways to think about this topic; the one you choose will determine the medical-supplies portion of your always-carry kit. Most commuters figure that since they're in a city, help is always nearby in the event that they get run over. But if you're traveling outside metropolitan areas, pack large bandages (a half dozen four- by four-inch gauze compress pads) for those large-area surface scrapes that result from contact with the pavement, to stanch the flow and protect the wound while waiting for help.

Most crossover cyclists who sometimes spend weekends on country roads or trails simply add a lunch to their everyday bag of bike gear and head out. You may tell yourself you'll always remember to add your medical supplies, but chances are you'll forget now and again. You don't want to be caught in the wilds without any first-aid gear.

I suggest, therefore, that you glance at the following list, add to or delete from it as you wish, seal the contents in a zip-lock bag and then inside a ripstop nylon bag (preferably of a bright color, and labeled appropriately with a waterproof marker), and carry it with you always.

For those of you who feel you've satisfied your medical requirements by purchasing one of the numerous 'biker's first-aid kits,' do yourself a favor by adding the bandages mentioned above if yours is lacking in this area. I am continually amazed at the paucity of bandages such kits contain; perhaps those who put them together have never seen the amount of skin that can be lost in seconds. As preventive care is always preferable to first-aid application, ride carefully, defensively, on both road and trail.

My first-aid kit:

sunblock

ibuprofen/aspirin

butterfly closure bandages (think of these as "Band-Aid stitches")

adhesive bandages (various sizes)

gauze compress pads (a half dozen 4" × 4")

gauze (1 roll)

an Ace bandage or Spenco joint wrap

Benadryl (an antihistamine to guard against allergic reactions, for trail riding and touring)

water purification tablets (tetraglycine hydroperiodide tablets, marketed under the more easily pronounced names of Portable Aqua, Coughlan's, Globaline)

moleskin or Spenco Second Skin

hydrogen peroxide/iodine/Mercuro-chrome   (some kind of antiseptic)

snakebite kit (read the directions *before* you are bitten*)

tweezers

It should be obvious that you will have to repack some of these items (like the water purification tablets, which come in a small but heavy glass jar). I prefer using watertight plastic 35 mm film canisters. (Note: Do not use a clear film canister for the water purification tablets. These are apparently adversely affected by exposure to light.)

It is only human nature to have every intention in the world to put together your own kit—and then not do so. I've seen this with fellow riders for years. And so I'm going to suggest that you commuters and short-trail riders consider the Crash Pack First Aid Kit (endorsed by several mountain bike magazines, plus police departments and many other government workers; see appendix for the 800 number), which costs *very* little and yet has crammed into a zip-lock bag the size of a bike glove all the following (I list

---

* For cactus-country tours and even weekend desert rides, as well as mountain bike trips through jungles overseas, I remove the snakebite kit from my medical bag and keep it closer to me. It is, after all, one item you'll want to reach in a hurry.

these items here so you can compare them with my kit, and add or subtract as you wish):

- 6 adhesive bandages
- 3 extra-large bandages for knee and elbow
- 4 knuckle bandages
- 2 butterfly bandages
- 2 medium gauze pads (3" × 3")
- 2 large gauze pads (4" × 4")
- 2 medium Telfa pads
- 2 large Telfa pads
- 1 3M micropore surgical tape
- 4 Mycitracin Plus antibiotic ointment
- 1 Cortaid cream
- 6 BZK antiseptic wipes (benzylkonium chloride)
- 1 Natrapel insect repellent
- 2 After Bite wipes
- 2 Motrin 2's
- 1 Finish Line citrus gel hand cleaner

Crash Pack.

If you plan to spend a lot of time in the backcountry, note the information in chapter 5 on the Madden Mountaineering Off-Road Emergency Kit, which is both a first-aid *and* a survival kit.

▪ CAR RACKS ▪

For many people, the trailheads and day trips start hundreds of miles from home. To transport you and your bike safely, a car rack is a great investment.

Your choice of racks will be determined by placement, i.e. where you want the bikes to sit (on the roof, behind the vehicle, or standing upright in a truck bed); speed of attachment (some roof rack mounts require removal of the bicycle's front wheel); number of bikes to be transported; and, of course, cost. Once again you will have to play the wise consumer, as finding the perfect rack for your car or truck is made difficult by the number of choices and considerations.

The least expensive option, back-of-car racks, have improved immeasurably in the last decade, but your automobile will nevertheless be subjected to at least a chance of being scraped from pedal or handlebar unless you invest in one of the very expensive (but very stable) hitch-mounted racks. A couple of these now pivot out of the way; not being able to open a trunk or hatchback with the bike or bikes attached has always been a drawback of rear-mount racks. Other drawbacks are the amount of dust the

Back-of-car rack.

Roof Rack.

bikes pick up while on dirt roads, the danger of striking the wheels on the road when hitting holes or high bumps, and blowing the tire if you aren't careful to keep it away from the exhaust.

No matter where you ultimately decide to carry your bike, be sure to lock it to the rack—and the front wheel to the rack or frame—when you leave the vehicle. And, for heaven's sake, if you choose a roof rack model, remember when there's a bike on the roof. I had always prided myself on never doing what almost everyone else I know has done at one time or another: crashed their bikes into garage roofs or McDonald's drive-up windows, or some other sloppy move. And then, last fall, while driving down the dirt road in Arkansas that leads to the Womble Trail, I failed to spy a single low limb jutting out across the road. It peeled my Cannondale like an apple. Took me almost an hour to retrue the rear wheel enough so I could ride it.

▪ TOOLS ▪

In the industrywide move toward miniaturization, tool manufacturers have not stood aside. It is now possible to obtain any number of multipurpose minitools that fit into a pocket, weigh a couple hundred grams, and offer several sizes of Allen wrenches, two or three box wrenches, flat and Phillips screwdrivers, a chain tool, a spoke wrench, and perhaps a pedal wrench and crank bolt wrench, and other doodads to boot.

However, do not simply assume that everything you'll possibly need is lurking within your minitool. Check the size of each and every Allen head bolt on your bike; if your minitool doesn't offer each one, you'll need to buy the missing Allen wrenches to pack along. Study those bolt-and-nut combinations and other parts of your bike where it might be necessary to possess a second wrench to hold one piece from turning while your minitool grips the other.

The following is a good all-around commuting/trail riding/touring tool kit, guaranteed to handle just about anything that can go wrong with your bike. Read it, subtract those items duplicated by a minitool (if you go the minitool route, that is), then add or subtract or substitute items according to your particular kind of riding and desired level of preparedness and riding weight.

Tire levers*

Spare tube *and* patch kit*

Air pump*

Allen wrenches (3, 4, 5, and 6 mm)

Six-inch crescent (adjustable-end) wrench

Small flat-blade-tip screwdriver

Chain rivet tool

Spoke wrench (make sure it fits *your* spokes)

Channel locks (six-inch handles)

Air gauge

Extra Schrader tube valve cap (metal kind, with valve-stem remover) or Presta valve cap (whichever you'll need)

Baling wire (ten-inch length; good for temporary repair if something big breaks)

Duct tape (small five-foot roll; good for temporary repair if something small breaks, can also be used as tire boot if nothing better is present)

Boot material (small piece of old sew-up tire works best; large tube patch is a good substitute)

Spare chain link

Rear derailleur pulley

Spare nuts and bolts (especially rack-mounting bolts)

Paper towel and tube of waterless hand cleaner

For my longer, heavily laden rides I add to the list extra spokes, freewheel tool and pocket vise (or chain whip or Cassette Cracker, whichever tool is required to replace broken spokes on the freewheel side), cone wrenches, and cotterless crank removal tools.

* These items are the minimum you should carry at all times if you're a commuter, or out for a single-day trip.

▪ WORK STAND ▪

On the road there is little choice but to flip a bike on its back to do repairs. Learn how and when to lubricate, and a few points of preventive maintenance (see chapter 7), and chances are you'll never experience a bad breakdown. But you will, however, have to adjust your derailleur now and again. The beefy cables probably won't break, but they will stretch. And for this operation (a surprisingly easy one once you get the hang of it), as for general bike and chain cleaning, it is easiest to work while the bike is upright and the rear wheel is lifted free from the ground. The answer—a work stand.

Least expensive of all alternatives are what bike shops call display stands. These are simple, two-legged, twisted pieces of steel that wrap around the down tube on one end and support the bottom bracket at the other. Considerably more costly, and a world apart in working comfort, is the Blackburn Work-Stand and its look-alikes. The Blackburn's 360-degree rotating jaws hold both wheels off the ground, making tune-ups even easier. And the entire stand folds up to hide easily beneath a bed or in a closet.

CHAPTER 3

RIDING TECHNIQUE

Some time ago, while laboring through Henry James's seemingly interminable novel *The Golden Bowl*, I read a single-line critique of the author's style that has remained with me ever since, and it comes to mind as I begin this chapter: "Nuance, nuance—nothing but nuance!" *Webster's* defines the word nuance as "a slight or delicate variation, a shade of difference," which describes perfectly the problem of discussing riding technique on a mountain bike. I can provide the basics of saddle position during climbs and descents, of pedal position when riding trails, of how to lift one's wheels across a water bar or jump over a ditch. But there is nothing like time on the bike to teach you the delicate handling techniques required on tough terrain.

▪ CLIMBING ▪

The general movement of mountain bike frame geometry—from the very relaxed angles of the early '80s to the somewhat steeper angles and shorter chainstays of today (shorter chainstays place the rider's weight more directly over the rear wheel)—means easier climbing on steep roads and trails. But no matter how old a bike you own, you'll benefit from a momentary analysis of body position during a climb.

In essence, climbing on a mountain bike is a matter of power, endurance, and balance. If the hill is too steep or your legs and arms too weak, or if you are good for bursts of speed but not aerobically fit for longer pulls, even the best of riding styles will not take you to the top. Conversely, *power*—the kind of full-body, anaerobic effort seldom required in thin-tire recreational cycling—and *endurance*—the ability to keep all systems going for long mountain climbs—serve only to *help* you win a summit. A poor riding style requires a great deal more effort to make it up a hill. Why? Because the third ingredient, *balance,* is the key to transmitting that power and endurance into front-wheel contact and rear-wheel traction.

We all learned one kind of balance as kids, the kind required to keep us from falling off the bike to the right or left. The balance needed to make it up a hill involves the other direction—forward or back. Simply, when going up a steep hill one must balance between the need for one's body weight to be over the rear wheel for traction and the necessity of leaning forward so as to hold the front end to the ground.

It seems plain enough. Just keep the body in a straight line over the bike, lean forward for increased leg propulsion and let some of your upper-torso weight assist the arms in keeping the front end down, and shift forward or back in the saddle as required to maintain traction and front-end contact. That is, when you feel the rear wheel slipping a bit, you know it requires more weight upon it; shift back a bit in the saddle. As the hill grows more steep and the front end tries to lift, you know it's time to apply weight there to keep it down.

Well, the *theory* is simple enough but the execution is far more complex, especially when the steepness of the hill appears to require your weight in both the front and the rear at the same time. What can be done?

One option is to leave the saddle (not to walk; that's the last option, and we're not quite to it yet) to gain more power momentarily from the standing position and, by leaning forward, to hold the front end down. Tim Metos, my model for this technique (and owner of Wild Rose Mountain Sports in Salt Lake City), describes this technique as "scissoring"—using the body's far greater mass (five or six times that of the bike) and the momentum gained by standing up to lurch the bike forward with the arms over a particularly steep section, then returning quickly to a sitting position if greater traction is required by the rear wheel.

Much more can be written about climbing technique, but you will learn the nuances far more quickly by spending time in the saddle. I'll add only the suggestions that you outfit your bike with very low gears, learn to anticipate the need for a lower gear and to shift into it *before* you begin straining at the pedals (derailleurs don't like being shifted at such high-torque moments; they respond sloppily), and realize that power, endurance, and balance are acquired only over time.

▪ DESCENDING ▪

Descents on a thin-tire bike are pure pleasure and little work; all you have to do is steer. On fat tires the pleasure is sometimes ratcheted upward to that of white-knuckled delight. Unfortunately, the work quotient is also increased—first by the hand and forearm strength required to slow your speed to one approaching some degree of safety, and second by a need to apply those riding techniques necessary to keep from catapulting over the handlebars.

The first thing to learn before trying tough descents is which brake lever operates which brake. Usually, but not always, the left lever works the front brake. Most of us learned years ago that it is a good idea while riding with hand brakes to apply both at the same time. Hit the brakes while riding down a steep hill on a bike (any bike) and you'll feel your body wanting to continue moving forward in the saddle; we intuitively use our arms and legs to counteract this tendency by pushing ourselves back in the saddle, and thereby keep the rear wheel on the ground. Mechanically the front brake is applying more stopping power; the rear brake is helping slow the overall speed, as well as working with your backward body shift to keep your rear wheel and you from becoming airborne.

Now transfer this scenario to an *extremely* steep road or trail over rough terrain (when roads are paved they are usually made more moderate in grade by the engineers), and things become more complicated:

1. Maintain your normal, relatively upright/somewhat forward position in the saddle and you'll pitch over the bars.
2. Fail either to lower your saddle height (and thereby your center of gravity), or to drop your rear end off the back of the saddle, and you'll pitch over the bars.
3. Attempt to steer laterally around an obstacle with your front brake locked as tightly as your rear brake and you'll pitch over the bars.

Sounds painful? Well, so too is a bad flip off the high dive, a poorly executed telemark, and a not-quite-high-enough pole vault. They all take practice, and the beforehand smarts to start off on smaller challenges. (Obviously, wearing a helmet at these times is a must.) Here are some techniques that will help you avoid the above mistakes.

Tim, "picking a line."

Body Position

In the photo to the left Tim Metos has assumed the proper slightly out-of-the-saddle (similar to that of a jockey in the stretch), three-and-nine-o'clock pedal position necessary for a descent. (If you keep one foot or the other close to the ground (six o'clock) you are at greater risk of your foot or the pedal striking an object, and propelling you out of the saddle or at least off your chosen path.)

In this photo Tim is "picking a line"—sitting up in the saddle to see far ahead and choosing his path of descent. You already know this technique if you run rivers—that exciting, apprehensive moment when you round the bend, focus on the rapids out ahead, and must choose your path over them.

In the photo to the right you see Tim going over a large rock on the descent. As he approached it he shifted his weight back in the saddle to let the unweighted front end climb easily up and over. If this were level terrain, he would have then shifted his weight forward to allow an unweighted rear-end hop over the obstacle, thereby producing slight contact and avoiding a pinched tube or damage to the rim. On this steep descent, however (which by the way is much steeper than it appears in the photo), his weight must remain back in the saddle to counteract the grade. Rear wheel damage in this instance is avoided by extremely slow speed.

By shifting weight to the rear, Tim allows the unweighted front wheel to climb easily over the rock.

Brakes

More important than body position, however, is braking.

Notice too that knees and elbows remain somewhat bent, to act as shock absorbers and allow more fluid movement. Another point: If it became obvious that gravity was winning out, Tim would have attempted to separate himself from the bike, dropping it beneath him preferably on the nonderailleur side and hopping off to safety.

The photo on the next page shows master carpenter and bike racer Brian Thurgood of Salt Lake City flying downhill in the position required if you choose not to lower your saddle. Remember that great skill is necessary to hang this far rearward and still steer safely. Remember, too, that an IQ of about 6 is required to race down a mountain without a lid.

In the photo of Tim on page 70, the rear is being applied, but the front is being feathered (the same action one does with the gas pedal when try-

ing to start a car on a very cold day), because locking it up will not only cause him to pitch forward but will also deny him the ability to change directions right or left. Learning to let go— acquiring that speed necessary to roll over obstacles or change directions while descending—is one of the hardest techniques to master.

Position necessary for flying down a hill when seatpost has not been lowered.

Note: I asked Tim Metos about his preference in tires, thinking that since he owns a bike shop he has probably tried every bike in the book. He says he likes riding with two different treads—a more aggressive tread in front, a tire that rolls better in the rear. His reasoning: "The body tends to follow the front wheel, so if it washes out first and the back wheel hangs, you tend to pitch around sideways. In this case the body starts leading the bike rather than the bike leading the body. If, on the other hand, the rear wheel washes out, you tend to hang on to the bars and are still following the bike, which is easy to correct." Don't worry if Tim's words are clear as mud. Once you're in the saddle you'll *feel* exactly what he means.

■ AVOIDING OBSTACLES ■

On a dirt road or wide path the rider has the option of moving around an obstacle. On narrow single-tracks, however, they must be negotiated in other ways.

Below Sarah Bennett, mountain bike guide author, is demonstrating avoidance by leaning the bike sharply away from the obstacle, and counterbalancing by leaning the body in the opposite direction. In this deep and narrow single-track she has little wiggle room, and even if she still strikes the object, it will be but a glancing blow.

Counterbalancing to avoid an obstacle.

But let's say the obstacle runs completely across the path, such as in the case of a water bar. Water bars are earth or wooden trenches that funnel mountain runoff across a trail. They often are raised many inches above the path surface, and will cause wheel damage or a fall if not negotiated carefully.

Now, the easiest option in crossing a water bar (or a curb) is simply to lift the front wheel. Pedal at slightly reduced speed to a point just before the water bar, slide back in the saddle, and—at the same time—lift up on the handlebars and push them forward. The momentum gained will allow the front wheel to become airborne over the water bar or curb, or at least will allow the front wheel to roll over it effortlessly. Now the task is to move the rear wheel across the obstacle with as little contact as possible. This is effected by a quick transference in body weight—once the front wheel is

Hop over without either wheel touching the ground.

safely over—toward the front of the bike. When done correctly the rear wheel "floats" across.

A second technique for clearing across-the-path obstacles is similar to the wheelie just described, thought the attempt here is to hop over without either wheel touching. In this case you'll need a bit more speed, then almost the same moves as above. Once airborne, however, the body weight must be transferred forward even more dramatically and the handlebars pushed downward; the hoped-for reaction is for the rear wheel to soar over whatever is being jumped. Remember to keep the front wheel perfectly straight when hitting the ground, as an angled wheel can cause a bad spill.

Tim demonstrates the beginning move in a static jump in the left-hand photo on the next page, a method of crossing an obstacle when you haven't had the opportunity to gain momentum. Notice that he has compressed himself on the bike much as he might if beginning to jump while standing: knees bent, body in a crouch, ready to spring upward.

To the right you see him executing a moving leap, again from a compressed position, but this time using the momentum of forward movement to help pull the bike from the ground. His feet in the clips lift the rear of the bike; his hands lift the front end.

Beginning move in a static jump.

Executing a moving leap.

Other obstacles must be negotiated with similar planning and skill. Narrow ditches can be jumped. Wide, shallow ditches can be ridden straight across if the walls aren't steep, or at an angle if they are. Wide, deep ditches act upon your bike and you as tank traps do on tanks. Be careful. And shallow streams can be crossed if taken at good speed, once you have reconnoitered them for depth, of course. I assume that your sensitivity to the environment, as well as your desire not to increase the number of areas from which mountain bikes are excluded, means you are only riding streams at spots where they cross roads and trails. I trust, too, that you aren't locking your rear wheel during descents in soft soil, thereby causing ruts, or chewing up fallen logs by bashing them with chain rings while attempting jumps. Much more on this in chapter 6.

> Note: On technical descents (downhill runs through rough terrain), a hop is not an option to clear obstacles, because one must maintain contact with the ground to maintain control.

▪ STARTING OFF ON A HILL ▪

Any number of things can cause you to "lose" a hill, and if you don't know how to get started again you'll be spending a lot of time walking to the top. The following technique is especially useful when you've stopped on a steep grade. If you aren't already in a very low gear, move your shift lever a bit, lift

Starting position for hill-climbing.

The left leg searches for the pedal as the right leg continues its propulsion.

The left foot locating the pedal.

The left foot is in the clip and ready to pedal.

the rear wheel and pedal with your other hand or foot and continue to do this until you manage to jump your chain into the proper sprockets.

The first photo shows Tim in the starting position: left foot on the ground, right foot on the pedal, body leaning forward. He is rocking back and forth slightly, as one might on a swing to gain momentum, then will simultaneously push off with the left leg and push down with the right.

The left leg rises up to begin its search for the pedal, as the right leg continues its propulsion. If his left foot has not found the pedal by the time his right pedal reaches six o'clock, he'll have to stop and try again.

The shot taken a moment later shows the left foot very close to locating the left pedal. In the last photo in the series Tim is successfully in the clips and straps, standing in the pedals and leaning forward to increase momentum.

▪ CARRYING THE BIKE ▪

This is usually not an option for me. With all the weight I normally pack, it's either ride or push. But chances are you'll be pedaling a far lighter rig, and so you should know how to portage.

Several companies offer carry straps, slings, and pads designed specifically for comfort when packing a bike along on your shoulder. When used, the bike's handlebars point in the same direction that you walk; the pedal is tucked either forward or back of the torso.

Many bikers don't care for pads that attach to the bike, as on some frames they take up the space that could be occupied by a water bottle. And, as Tim shows, they are not needed for comfortable portaging on trails wide enough to allow you to carry the bike sideways.

In the top-left photo on the next page Tim uses his foot to push the left pedal into the nine-o'clock position.

After hoisting the bike up by the top tube with his right hand (shown in the top-right photo on the next page), Tim reaches through the main frame triangle and grabs the handlebars while his left hand holds the saddle.

The pedal is tucked to the side of the hip, the crankarm rests comfortably against the small of the back, and the top tube lies across the shoulders. In this position (shown in the bottom photo on next page) you can carry the bike easily for a great distance, as well as maneuver the bike's front and rear wheels around obstacles (through the control provided by your grip on both the saddle and the handlebars). You now have enough riding tips to begin your own trail work. Start off small, don't be impatient, do be careful.

4

URBAN JUNGLES: COMMUTING ON TWO WHEELS

The mountain bike is without doubt the very best commuting machine known to man. They're better than streetcars and bullet trains, buses and automobiles, subways and els. They go anywhere. They go anytime. They don't leave a mess in the street, like horses. They don't pollute the air, or refuse to start, or react to oil shortages. They scoff at city transit workers' strikes. Nothing short of massive snowstorms will stop them (a time when mountain bikers, in shape from their two-wheeled commuting, can swap wheels for snowshoes or cross-country skis and still make it to the office or factory). And all this for what car insurance costs you for a year.

Cycling to work and back is economical, good exercise, and environmentally sound. Yes, cold days will feel colder (until you've warmed up after a few blocks), and hot days hotter, when you start them on two wheels. But I can promise you that you'll appreciate the warm cup of coffee and the first cool hint of coming autumn far more when you have known their opposites. And although evening low-light commutes in winter require far more caution, you will find there is something romantic about knowing each phase of the moon. You'll notice birdsong and the first buds in spring, and the more expansive mood of crossing guards when you say hello to them face to face—not through a windshield.

You will also get to know your city better, as you learn the side streets and alternate routes through parks. True, your commute in all but the most traffic-jammed cities (where bikers regularly *beat* cars in crosstown races) will probably take more time. But you have to factor in the jog or trip to the gym you won't have to take, and the extra hours you won't have to work because of the money you've saved by biking. And that's not adding in the fact that you've changed the chore of commuting into something that most people say is sorely missing from their lives—adventure.

Approach two-wheeled commuting as you would any adventure—with respect and concern for safety. Most riders will think a bit before hitting the trails; they venture forth with a veteran who can teach them the moves, analyze their mistakes, and work up to fast descents on rough terrain. But not so with pedaling to work. With so little forethought it's a wonder that most of us keep from getting creamed.

First, remember you are not a car, and that motorists do recognize that you're a human on a bike, and worthy of at least a second thought. Your facial features and hand movements are much more visible than when you are sitting behind a wheel, increasing the opportunity for *personal* communication—human to human, not bike to car. Learn to use it to your advantage. A simple wave of thanks when you've been given the go-ahead, or a nodding mea culpa when you've pulled a bonehead move, will do much to make that motorist think kindly of the next cyclist who wanders into range.

I wrote in my first thin-tire book many years ago: "All the savvy of an animal in the bush is necessary to negotiate a business district without winding up as a hood ornament." Mountain bikes are infinitely safer commuting vehicles than their spindly, unstable cousins, but don't get cocky: ATBs and Buicks still aren't an even match. I learned that lesson the hard way.

▪ A COMMUTER'S BIKE ▪

The following is an annotated checklist to help you in your preparations before your initial ride to work.

Upswept Bars

Some cyclists prefer the head-up, traffic-watching position that these handlebars (found on some mountain bikes and almost all "city" bikes) allow. Or rather, that they *require*. Which is the problem I have with them. I prefer standard handlebars with long, curving bar ends attached, which allow an upright position when you want to assume it, and others that make trail riding and touring so much more comfortable. Regardless of your handlebar setup, it's critical to learn

Bike commuter, Salt Lake City, Utah.

those handlebar positions that allow the fastest reaction time *and* greatest views possible.

My favorite for both fast downtown commuting and fast or technical single-tracking is this: thumb and forefinger wrapped securely around the handlebar in a place where the thumb can reach the gear-shift lever; the remaining three fingers rest upon the brake lever. This position of thumb and forefinger will keep the bars from being jerked out of your hands when you hit a chuckhole or sewer grating (something you must watch for like a hawk; call the city streets department to report those gratings with metal bars set so wide as to engulf bike tires), and will allow instantaneous braking when something pulls out in front of you. Like a bus.

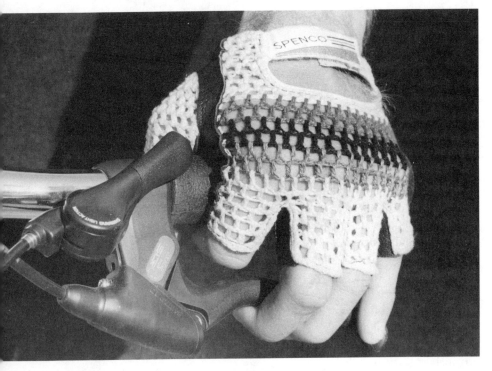

A good grip postion.

Rearview Mirror

A must. I've discussed my favorite kind earlier (see page 35), but will repeat that especially when commuting, you don't want a mirror that shows little of what's behind you, nor a mirror you have to look for.

Handlebar Bells and Horns—A handlebar bell (like Mirrycle's Incredibell) is a civilized way to communicate with pedestrians. It's the audible but unspoken equivalent of a mild "Excuse me" when moving past someone in a crowded hallway. Compressed-air horns, on the other hand, communicate something like GET OUT OF THE WAY!! when used on pedestrians. So you shouldn't be surprised when some poor sap trying to cross a street reacts to you as *you* do when blasted by a car's horn.

Compressed-air horns are excellent, however, for communicating with motorists in those few crisis instances when other means (hand signals or a shout, for instance) will not work. They are also good for commuters who wish to alert a neighborhood and thereby, one hopes, stop an approaching

CycleAware CycleHorn DBX.

Handlebar bell mounted on bike.

mugger in his tracks. (But women take note: No horn in existence will bring the response that a woman's scream will. The combination is sure to gain attention.)

One innovative bike products company, CycleAware, has developed a "multi signal electronic bicycle horn" that is powered by a 9-volt battery and emits your choice of a "friendly passing signal," an emergency siren, or a very loud blast. (Though to my ears this loudest squawk is a somewhat less bloodcurdling blast than that produced by compressed-air horns.) I like its quick-release handlebar mounting bracket, and especially the fact that it can be activated either by depressing the button on the horn itself or by a remote button on the grip, which means you don't have to let go of your brake handle to hit the horn. The "friendly" signal is, unfortunately, still not as friendly as a bell, but that's a price perhaps worth paying in order to have the louder-blast option at your fingertip. If you ride crowded rail-trails (abandoned railroad tracks now converted to trails for human-powered travel) a lot, however, I suggest you remain with a bell. No one likes getting blasted electronically even by a lower-volumed horn, and chances are that on rail-trails you'll be passing the same folks when you pedal back to the trailhead. Too many frowns and muttered comments can ruin a perfect day.

Which brings us back to my first choice in bells. There are two kinds of Incredibells—one that fits into the end of your handlebar or bar end, a second that mounts around either of those bars. These tiny beauties weigh in at an ounce, can be positioned for thumb or finger engagement, have no moving parts to rattle about, and offer the rider a range of volumes, from surprisingly loud to very gentle.

Tires

I've already discussed these in detail (see page 39), but in general I would suggest as high a pressure and as thin a tire as your roads will allow. Long distances and good roads would make me opt for 1.25-inch or 1.5-inch slicks or internal tread, with a top-end psi range of 90 or 100. Tires should be Kevlar belted or you should use tire liners or Slime. For me there's no better all-around commuting tire than the internal-tread-design 45–95 psi 26 × 1.25-inch Avocet Cross Kevlar Clincher, whose wide air pressure range makes it perfect as well for dirt roads and hard-packed nontechnical single-track trails and thus *the* tire for tours in which you might ride everything. (Why these have to cost as much as some car tires, however, is a mystery to me. The Performance Bicycle mail-order company has produced its own internal-tread Kevlar version—the AT-X—at half the price, but I avoid them due to their lack of a high-pressure range—45–60 psi only.) You might prefer the Avocet Cross in 1.25-inch width for faster touring and commuting, or the 1.9-inch for inclement weather commutes.

For commuting in snow, you'll need big knobbies. And don't forget the tire chains for icy days. Your local shop might not stock them, but you can order (or you can mail-order) the Pit Bull Mud Magnums that fit all knobbies of 1.95 inches to 2.1 inches. Chains by other companies are no doubt on their way, along with additional entries in the studded-tire market. I've even read how to "stud your own" tires for winter travel. But the fellow pictured in the magazine article looks like far more of a mechanic than I do. I'll stick with chains.

Fenders

Full wrap and as wide as they come if you want to keep completely dry, as I said in chapter 2, or snap- or Velcro-on/off plastic partials will do if the weather's not too wet. If you use your commuting bike for trail riding on weekends or after work, you might want to split the difference and go for the partials. On wet days I suggest you wear whatever you don't mind getting moist and pack your presentables (the term I always used, when commuting daily to work, for the clothes I wore to teach) in a pannier.

Pedals

Be sure they're large enough to handle the lightweight boots, or the shoe/shoe-cover combination, that you'll want for cooler and wet-weather commutes. Add rear reflectors to your pedals. If you decide to pedal in your leather dress shoes, protect the toes from scuffing by wrapping the inside of the toe clips with fabric or tape. Even the unbreakable plastic clips I use will scuff leather after a while. And if you're committed to your clipless pedals and accompanying footwear, just leave your work shoes at work or toss them in a pannier. A number of top-of-the-rack bags also have zippered compartments especially for shoes.

Gearing

Review my remarks in earlier chapters (see pages 19 and 29) on why I feel mountain bikes are poorly geared for fast commuting. If you often find yourself going too fast to pedal while on pavement, you might want to make the necessary adjustments to your drivetrain.

Water Bottles—and Dogs

I carry one bottle filled with water on commutes, and a second filled with straight ammonia. I use the ammonia to ward off the gauntlet of man's best friends who love to chase bikes. One good sniff of the stuff will usually send them away, and if you overshoot and get some in their eyes it will wash out without damage. I've only had to squirt a dozen dogs or so out of the millions who have taken it into their craniums to chase me. If I can manage to outride them—safely, without swerving into traffic—I do so.

I can often stop an attack (when I have the time) by halting, slapping my thigh, and calling out "Here boy" a couple of times. I never do this, of course, if such action would entice the dog to cross a busy road.

Like most people, I love to pet dogs and do so when they'll come to me on my commutes and tours, and as a result I have memories of mutt encounters from around the world. So don't reach immediately for your bottle of ammonia or can of HALT! (the aerosol repellent used by letter carriers, and something to use on tour when you need all your bottles for water). You might be ending a beautiful friendship before it's begun. And even if the bark is stern and the pursuit constant, I always attempt to end things with a commanding shout. Before the teeth, however, I douse 'em.

The CamelBak water bag will work to keep you hydrated on your city rides, of course, if your commute is long enough to justify the weight. Or you could go the route of hot or cold liquids at your fingertips through the insulated water bottles or vacuum bottles wedded to special steel cages (like the Ibis Hot Unit).

Racks

A rear rack will satisfy the needs of almost all commuters, but if you pack a great deal to work and back, or decide to go shopping on your way home, you might find a front rack convenient. Again, see chapter 2 (page 46) for details, including information on the ingenious Headland Utility X Rack, which attaches to the seatpost and has a weight limit of forty pounds. It's perfect for mounting a stuffed rack pack, but its placement rules out panniers.

Packs

Vagabond Outfitters now offers a large garment bag guaranteed to keep your work clothes wrinkle-free. As with the garment bags travelers lug onto planes, one's shirt, sport coat, dress, or skirt can be hung inside the Vagabond Outfitter's model and zippered closed. You lather up all you want in your Lycra getting a great workout across the city.

Somewhat less particular, I managed to get by with my carefully folded shirt and sport coat in one pannier, my books and notes and commuting kit (tools, rain gear, first-aid pack) in a second. One or two panniers seems in fact the choice of most who wheel to work, and a backpack the most desired bag for college students pedaling to campus.

I commuted during my teaching days with the same panniers I used for touring. Most of you will probably prefer a smaller bag, but if not, skip ahead to chapter 5 for information on touring packs. If you have not so much to carry, refer to chapter 2 (page 55) on fanny packs, messenger bags, rack packs/duffels, briefcases, shopping basket panniers, seat bags, handlebar bags, and then read here about backpacks. I'll provide some details about one that is very popular with riders (Madden) and add a photo about another company's excellent pack (OverLand Equipment). You can look up the companies in the appendix and call or write for catalogs, and then see how others compare.

Pannier with groceries.

Madden Mountaineering's Abu— At a single glance you'll know this bag wasn't built to haul books around campus. One look at the tough eleven-ounce Cordura fabric, the extra wide and thick and *dense* shoulder straps, the full-length mesh ventilator back pad and the roomy fifteen-hundred-cubic-inch main bag capacity, and you'll know it was intended for the wilds. Okay, so you can take it there on weekends. In the meantime it will handle more than you'll ever need to carry, and if you're lucky it will hug you in the saddle as well as mine hugs me. A sternum strap and waist belt help keep the pack from going its own way around tight turns, or bouncing during rough descents. And the flexible framesheet allows a far more fluid feel to the load. (Riding with *in*flexible frames feels more like you're rolling your spine across a pine floor.) There's a wide, nearly flat shovel pocket across the face that's perfect for pens and calculators. The zipper tabs are enormous, so you'll never be hunting around for them with gloves on, and inch-wide zipper flaps keep out the rain. One suggestion, however: Put a few turns of duct tape around the zipper pulls, or paint on rubberizing compound, like Dip It. I want to hear the sounds of the city during my commuting, and the birds while I'm on trails—not zippers jangling together.

Rain Covers

Ponchos for bike bags. Buy them if you're interested in keeping your panniers dry. Yes, plastic bags *inside* your saddlebags will protect the contents,

Rain cover for pannier.

but the bags themselves will still be soaked. Some pannier manufacturers do not, amazingly, offer waterproof covers for their bags. If you need some very durable and very bright covers, head to Madden Mountaineering of Boulder, Colorado. Their bright orange covers are so visible that I've even stopped to put them on during particularly gray winter days when pedaling home at dusk. It was like donning two huge reflectors.

Pumps

Choose one short enough to fit inside (not stick out of, for this makes putting a pannier cover over the bag a pain) your ever-present commuting bag. The alternative is to mount the pump on your bike, which means you have one more thing to carry away from the bike each time you stop.

Saddle

I need only add to my remarks in chapter 2 that you remember to secure your saddle and seatpost when locking your bike at work. And that you plug the exposed hole in the seat tube if you remove the seatpost.

Lights

I was doing a catalog photo shoot for Blackburn/Bell Sports in California, and one of the models was a pleasant fellow (and a hell of a mountain biker) named Robert Choy. It was not until some time later that I learned I'd met the Henry Ford of flashing lights, the very fellow who designed and invented what I and a zillion other two-wheeled commuters have used for years to let motorists know where we are. Because of this meeting I'm now partial to VistaLites when it comes to the lightning-bug approach to after-dark safety, but no matter the brand buy a flasher for your rear. I prefer flasher taillights that run on AA batteries and are waterproof, though I forgo this for the helmet-mount model powered by a single AAA. Dusk and dawn are risky times to pedal, so I make it a practice to turn on my flashing tail-light long before dark on city streets. Besides, the batteries (especially the double A's) last almost forever; it's constant-discharge time—not intermit-tent—that drains the life out of the poor things.

I discussed up-front lights in chapter 2 (page 48), both the ones that let cars see you and those systems that allow you to see them—and the rest of the world—as well. If you aren't going to pack a light of some kind in your ever-present commuting bag, for safety's sake at the very least affix a flash-ing taillight to your helmet or bike. The helmet-mount VistaLite weighs a measly twenty-five grams, the bike-mount models a few ounces.

Locks

Review the discussion in chapter 2, then buy one or more for your bike, front wheel, and seatpost—and use them.

Two U-locks are advisable.

▪ A COMMUTER'S DRESS ▪

During my years as an urban commuter I usually rode to work in whichever pants and shirt I planned to teach in that day, and packed my tie and sport coat (folded once and slipped into a plastic bag, it fit nicely in a pannier and didn't wrinkle). On very warm days it took only a minute to fold my dress shirt as would a professional laundry, then pack it in a bike bag by itself; I then pedaled in a T-shirt and jettisoned the thing upon reaching school. On very hot days I pedaled slowly so as not to work up a great sweat, and took five minutes in the bathroom to strip to the waist, wipe down with a washcloth, and add new deodorant if I thought it necessary. Presto—I was clean, and fully awake because of the exercise. I've never understood those folks who use the excuse that they can't ride to work because, they claim, "there's no shower facility." Granted, I'd feel I needed one if I jogged several miles to work. But even biking fifteen miles one way I never worked so hard that I couldn't feel completely refreshed after five minutes at a sink.

Female commuters who don't want to wear pants could opt for a "mixte" frame, in which the top tube runs parallel to the down tube and thus leaves room for a skirt (a stronger design than the traditional "girl's bike"). Or you could of course pedal in pants and change at work.

Bike Gloves/Regular Gloves

By all means, for the host of reasons given in chapter 2, you should ride in gloves. Come cool and cold weather you'll need to do more, however, than simply choose the color of riding glove, and the pair whose mesh weave leaves the most attractive tan pattern on the backs of your hands. My choice in early fall and late spring is a thin pair of poly liners worn inside the fingerless bike gloves. The combination is sufficiently warm, allows great finger dexterity, offers the required palm padding, and makes you look like you've just pedaled off the set of *Mad Max*. The cheapie cotton gardening gloves won't cut it for long commutes, they'll sweat up in no time and leave your fingers cold.

When summer is gone I add to the kit my bright red Outdoor Research (OR) Cordura and Gore-Tex Basic Mitt Shells. Though they're expensive, you don't have to be a sculptor or violinist to want to keep frostbite at bay. The shells come halfway to my elbows and can be cinched down both at the wrist and at the opening. Their waterproof/windproof capability make my hands so much warmer that it's usually almost winter before I need more protection from the cold than that provided by poly liners, bike gloves, and waterproof shells. When that time comes, I add the thickest ski gloves I own and cram these into the Gore-Tex shells. (The seams on my mitts are not taped and thus would not be waterproof had I not seam-sealed them with the same gunk we all use on tent seams—discussed in the next chapter. I wore them in an all-day 35-degree drizzle in Iceland after I seam-sealed them, and nary a drop made it in.)

Now, Outdoor Research also offers something it calls Rain Mitts. These are constructed of extremely thin Gore-Tex, and the seams are already taped. You might consider them if you need waterproof mitts to jog in as well, or if you play with a bike computer while riding; these gloves are reported to be thin enough to allow even the triggering of wristwatch dials and buttons.

And then there are the unique Madden Mountaineering Bullwinkles, cold-weather mountain bike mittens whose polypropylene linings add considerable warmth and that attach (get this!) *around* the handlebar, brake handle, and gear shift levers, yet allow the dexterity of individual fingers.

Finally, if you need a glove that can stand up to sub-zero conditions, try Outdoor Research's Expedition Modulars, with the Expedition Glove GT Liners inside. Yes, they're expensive. But then you won't have to invest in another pair when you decide to climb K2.

Pants Clips

Rubber bands work, but they have the habit of breaking when you've just relubed your chain and are wearing your best slacks. You have a choice of metal bands, or fabric strips (oftentimes reflective for night travel) with a Velcro patch to stay in place.

Pants clips are vital for commuters.

Poncho/Chaps or Rainsuit

Cyclists have a choice when it comes to staying dry: the poncho/chaps combination (or poncho and gaiters when the wind isn't blowing rain horizontally at you), or a rainsuit. I wear a rainsuit during midwinter commutes and on winter tours, and either the poncho/chaps or poncho/gaiters combination at all other times. The reason? Heat buildup inside a rainsuit. No matter the material, pedal hard inside a full rainsuit (top and bottom) and you'll feel like you're working out in a greenhouse. The best suits—made of Gore-Tex and fitted with a host of zippers and vents beneath each arm and across the back—are worlds apart from the old heavy nylon outfits, which had the smell of an oil rig and weighed a ton. Regulating your body temperature on a

Poncho for a rainy day.

bike is crucial, of course, for both comfort and performance, and these new rainsuits go far in allowing you to do so. But count on a suit to keep off the rain in summer and you'll be just as wet from your own sweat.

Bike ponchos, on the other hand, are designed to allow air to circulate around the body while still shedding rain. This works because of their unique design—pullover, tentlike, waterproof, with the back flap tying about the waist and the front equipped with thumb loops to stretch this portion out to the handlebars. With ponchos or rainsuits it is critical that the hood be large enough to fit over your helmet easily, so as not to restrict your ability to look about and to turn around when checking for traffic. You must also be able to cinch the hood tightly about the face—if this can't be done you'll lose your peripheral vision and greatly increase your chances of not getting to work at all.

When wearing a poncho, a hard or more horizontal rain (those days that remain in memory, when it comes in sheets blown by ferocious winds), or rain splashed up by passing motorists after a real downpour, can still soak one's lower torso. This is where the pants or chaps come in.

Look for snaps or Velcro closings when choosing rain pants and pay particular attention to pocket access and how comfortable they are around the waist. Also, remember that you can mix a top from one suit with the bottoms of another, if you prefer. Rain pants, however, close off the crotch and waist to airflow, causing dampness inside and hindering the freedom of pedaling somewhat. Chaps, in contrast, are simple waterproof tubes that tie at the waist to a belt loop, thereby allowing air to circulate. The chap bottoms overlap gaiters (the shoe coverings discussed next), which in turn overlap the open portions of shoes or boots. It is a system similar to roof tiles, with successive, rain-shedding layers.

> Note: Because the design of ponchos and chaps allows tremendous breathability, inexpensive fabric can be used. The K-Kote waterproofing can be restored with products such as Re-Kote and Flex-Dri, available in some outdoor shops and catalogs, so don't think you have to buy a new poncho/chaps outfit if yours begins to leak. Mind did after *six* years of hard use. It cost me three bucks and twenty minutes to restore it. I'll let you know if it ever wears out.

Another note: It once was easy to locate and purchase bike ponchos. Most companies have now stopped making them, however, and I assume for the following two reasons: (1) With so many bikers believing that speed and efficiency are all-important, the greater wind resistance of a poncho curtails sales; (2) Why sell relatively inexpensive ponchos to riders when you can convince them they need full-on Gore-Tex rainsuits and sell a product that costs ten times as much? While other companies might still offer them, the only place I can find bike ponchos is in the Campmor mail-order catalog (see appendix).

Gaiters/Rainboots/Waterproof Socks

Gaiters are designed to shed water away from the tops of boots or shoes. They usually wrap around the leg and close in the rear, the side, or best of all in front. I used a heavy wool lace-up-the-sides pair for some fifteen years and still cherish the things, but nothing compares to the ease of putting on and taking off a front-opening gaiter with a Velcro closing. For the past few years I've used the Outdoor Research Crocodiles that I purchased at the same time that I bought the waterproof overmitts, and have pedaled and snowshoed in them happily. I prefer the stiff, breathable Gore-Tex uppers (1000 denier) of this model, and because they reach to just below the knee they reduce the number of days that I'm forced to don my chaps.

Shedding water downward from your poncho and gaiters (or poncho/chaps/gaiters in warm-weather storms, and rainsuit/gaiters or rainsuit/overboots in winter) to a lightweight waterproof boot is fine if your dress shoes are waiting for you at work or packed inside a pannier. My system has always been to leave a pair of shoes at work, and ride with warm, stiff boots in winter and lighter, cooler, but still stiff low-cut shoes in warmer months. (Waterproof your boots with saddle soap, Sno-Seal, Nikwax, Aquaseal, or one of the other products. And while you're at it, don't forget the other leather that grows thirsty through the year: toe-clip straps, gaiter straps, gloves, and some saddles—though you'll have to remember to use a saddle cover until the lubricant is absorbed.)

However, if you prefer to pedal in your work shoes (excluding high heels, I imagine), you'll need to take several steps: (1) As suggested earlier, wrap metal and hard-plastic toe clips to avoid abrasions on good leather shoes; (2) obtain a pair of Spenco or other orthotics to stiffen the midsole for efficient and comfortable pedaling; and (3) wear rainboots or waterproof socks in foul weather.

Because the hands and feet are so far from the heart, they feel the cold (and especially the *wet* cold) of winter greatly. Even on the most frigid days my body core feels warm after just a few blocks of pedaling, but fingers and toes (and head, which we'll deal with next) must be better protected to feel as warm as your heat-generating trunk. Let that trunk cool down for a long period (stop pedaling for ten minutes or so), or fail to wear enough or to work hard enough in the saddle to keep your body warm, and you could be in trouble.

My rainboots are Madden Mountaineering's Hot Dogs! (made of heavy 11½-ounce Cordura) for when it's wet *and* cold, but when it's just the cold that has me hurting I prefer Gore-Tex socks. Neoprene socks are much less expensive, but if you pedal any distance at all your feet will be soaked by the time you get to work, unless it's the absolute bitterest of days.

A common problem in footwear is that too-thick socks are crammed into shoes or boots too small for the job. The point here is to find the happy medium between desired insulation and freedom of circulation, a chore made far less difficult by today's selection of excellent moisture-wicking warm socks (cotton absorbs perspiration and should not be worn; try wool, wool blends, or synthetics, or—if your feet are sensitive—a silk liner sock and then the heavier pair), Gore-Tex socks, windproof toe-clip covers, boots (large enough to accommodate two layers of socks worn in winter), and water- and windproof overboots.

Goggles

If you've ever caught a raindrop in the eye while pedaling you know there's pain involved. Not all that much, granted, but there's also an unavoidable closing of the lid and then, for a moment, impaired vision. Until just a few years ago I counted on my large-lensed Ambermatic sunglasses (Highway Patrol–type; I hoped they made me look like Jack Nicholson) to repel light rain. You can't wear regular sunglasses, of course, because the cloudy skies that bring the rain also reduce the sunlight. Then middle age brought the need for full-time eyewear, and so I was protected all the time from light rain and small snowflakes.

Come the storms, however, or snowflakes the size of Frisbees, you'll need to move to goggles. Or those very expensive wraparound, bubble-lidded sunglass systems with clear or yellow lenses when you need them. My preference for years has been the relatively inexpensive Kroop's Goggles (address in appendix). They are extremely light, they have vent holes to prevent fogging (I find I have to use fog-free solutions to the lenses of my own specs, however), and their leather binding provides a good seal around the eyes against the elements. My only complaint is that the plastic lenses scratch rather easily, but I remedy this by carrying the goggles in a nylon bag (any bag of nonabrasive fabric will do).

And while we're in the wet, let me add that if you're goggled *you* can see the world around you far better than most motorists can, trapped as they are behind streaked glass. So *don't assume that you're seen.* If it makes sense to drive defensively when you're behind the wheel, it's a *must* to ride defensively as well.

First-Aid Kits

In chapter 2 I discussed the first-aid kit I've carried for years, and the excellent and inexpensive little kit offered under the name of Crash Pack (toll-free number in the appendix). I also mentioned the Madden Mountaineering Off-Road Emergency Kit (discussed in detail in chapter 5). Put one of these in your commuting bag and *keep* it there.

Head Coverings

You've probably heard that 50 percent of the body's heat is lost through an uncovered head. Chances are good—at least I hope they are—that your head will at least be covered by a helmet. But helmets are designed to let the maximum amount of air *in* and heat *out,* exactly the opposite of what we need in winter. A few helmet manufacturers offer wind- and waterproof helmet covers, and at least one mail-order company now sells its own brand of Gore-Tex covers, all of which help greatly. Begin with this protection. But when the real cold hits you'll want some kind of beneath-the-helmet head liner as well.

Almost two decades ago I met the designer and manufacturer of the Roly caps I'd worn for years while hiking and biking. (These resemble the dapper caps worn by drivers of foreign sports cars; the design helps them stay in place when I'm hiking or when I've removed my helmet.) We've become friends, and now for a quarter of a century I've hiked in his thick, washable, wool sport caps, and ridden with one of his silk caps beneath a helmet when it's cool. Both models have earflaps (ears are especially vulnerable in the cold). The company's address is in the appendix.

But when very cold weather hits I switch to wool or wool-blend stocking caps beneath my helmet, and on the most frigid days I add an earband for greater insulation around the ears but also as protection against the "ice-cream headaches" I've gotten on the coldest days of my long tours and even shorter trail rides. Helmet liners of various wickable, insulating fabrics, and of a design that caps the forehead and covers the ears, are offered through many catalogs. Most trail riders I meet up with in winter, however, seem to stay warm enough in just their helmets and thick earbands. (Remember that the thicker the band, the more difficult it will be to tuck the top of it beneath the front lip of your helmet. The tendency is to want to cock back your helmet rather than adjust the strap, but wearing a helmet like a bonnet exposes your forehead to the hard knocks of life. Take the moment necessary to adjust things.)

If you're a motorist, covering the top of your head and maybe adding a pair of earmuffs is sufficient. But bikers must remember that their heads have other parts, and that these parts too are vulnerable to the cold. Page through a Campmor or Sierra Trading Post or Patagonia catalog (all addresses in the appendix), and you'll find headgear to cover all but your eyes.

Head coverings that fit snugly wont interfere with helmet fit.

There are balaclavas (which enclose the head, forehead, ears, neck, and chin, or chin plus mouth and nose); face masks of neoprene and other fabrics that cover all the face beneath the eyes and Velcro in place behind the neck (I prefer my fleece-lined neoprene model made by Gator; it's wonderfully comfortable and yet holds its shape and doesn't freeze to my beard); and neck gaiters of different lengths and fabrics (some riders like extralong neck gaiters that they can pull up around their faces when the need arises; I prefer the shorter models and separate face mask approach).

Jacket/Vest

You will notice that the heading of this section does not include the words "coats" and "parkas." This is because while a heavy coat would be comfortable (because of its warmth) for the first two or three blocks of your commute, it would make you miserably hot and sweaty after that. Your only way of cooling off would be to unzip a bit, which would be refreshing momentarily and freezing immediately afterwards. Your alternative, *the* first principle in cold-weather outdoor exercise, is to dress in layers.

Layers of loose, porous clothing create air pockets that trap the air warmed by your body (insulating layers), while a windproof outer garment of some kind keeps these air pockets from being replaced by cold air.

I therefore begin with long underwear (tops and bottoms both, of course) of a thin synthetic that will wick moisture from the skin (thereby avoiding the clammy feeling of cotton). Thin long underwear might at first sound completely out of place at work, but it makes great sense. The thick cotton union suits of old made one feel encumbered (as well as cold and clammy if any exercise was done), but thin underwear is like a second skin. Yes, red longjohns might look out of place with a skirt, but there are now non-Lycra fabric tights in every possible color. Catalogs, outdoor sports shops, and even some well-stocked bike shops will carry a number of fabrics by a host of different names that tout their wicking abilities, as well as the important benefit of not retaining odor.

Next comes winter Lycra tights for long commutes when I'm combining it with my workout (this is more often true for the back-to-home ride in the evening), or noncotton-blend slacks if the ride isn't long and I don't want to have to change at work. (Cotton pants will go shiny in the rear very quickly, and soon will wear out.) Most often the work pants are in the pannier, and I'm in a warm and embracing pair of winter brushed-polypro/Lycra tights. I miss pockets, and so I often wear a pair of black Patagonia Baggies (shorts) over the tights.

On the upper torso I don a noncotton shirt, usually a synthetic or wool blend. This is because the moisture drawn from the skin by the wicking underwear must have a layer to be wicked *to,* and if the next layer is cotton it will absorb it well but will simply remain wet. Next comes a synthetic sleeveless sweater, and while any will do wonders, my very strong preference is the kind that is breathable in back but which allows no wind to pass through the front. (Mine is the Patagonia Flyer, with a windproof front of P.E.F. fleece and a rear of Capilene.) This quality is of little importance when topped by the windproof jacket, but come the warmer days of early spring I find myself shoving the jacket in a pannier and pedaling with the vest as final layer. It's amazing how much warmer I am with a windblock across my front torso. I also choose the sporty model with a high zippered collar, as it takes the place of a neck gaiter. And if you avoid the expensive final outer layer of a parka (discussed next), I suggest a thick sleeveless sweater of synthetic fill beneath a lined waterproof shell. I chose this for my fall/winter three-month ride down the Rockies, and even on the coldest days felt like I was pedaling with my torso in a sleeping bag.

And now we come to what to wear on top, that final outer layer when it isn't raining or snowing but it's too cold for just the clothing we've donned thus far. The decision is easy for my midwinter hiking or snowshoeing trips, because the slow-moving exercise allows a far bulkier parka than I'd want on a bike. But outerwear for biking is a much more difficult decision.

If you're a jogger, you know how heavy or light an outer layer should be to keep you warm in winter. Until you stop, that is. The same is true for weekend road riding in the country, or trail riding when you really only have to stop when you make it back to your car. But urban-jungle bikers must figure a way not to sweat up too much while pedaling hard, yet not cool off too fast when the traffic lights and cars and pedestrians bring us to a halt. So what to wear?

Well, if you can afford it, you could go top-of-the-line with a Gore-Tex parka and zip-in fleece or other synthetic lining. Gore-Tex is reputedly far better than other less costly fabrics at the twin tasks of repelling water droplets from the outside and at the same time "breathing"—allowing water vapor molecules to escape. Now, you won't think "parka" when you see the "jacket" look of these; they are designed for fast-moving active sports and thus don't give the Michelin-man appearance. The bulky parka might be a good choice if you're in northern Minnesota or Montana or upstate New York, but elsewhere the lesser insulation is probably preferable. The removable lining of course extends the seasonal use of the parka (leaving you with a heavy rain jacket when it's zipped out), and also allows more freedom of movement while pedaling.

If you do choose a large parka, however, give some thought to the fill. I used a down-filled (duck- or goose-feather-filled) parka on my around-the-world ride, and it performed far more admirably than did my poor down sleeping bag (see the next chapter for that unhappy tale). Down holds its loft well but is difficult to launder properly *and* mats if it gets wet. So you'll need to be sure to keep it dry—from your water vapor inside and from water droplets or snowflakes outside—if you decide to commute in it. On the positive side, it will compress extremely well and thereby takes up little space in a pannier when not in use. On the downside (ho, ho), it's very costly.

Some commuters choose instead a Gore-Tex rainsuit top (with underarm zippered openings for ventilation) as their final outer layer even in winter, buying one large enough to fit over a pile or fleece sweater. For years

Commuter protected from
the winter cold.

I managed to commute just fine with an insulated jacket for warmth, and used the poncho/chaps/gaiters for rain and snow protection during winter. Gore-Tex is nice, but it isn't necessary.

Leg Warmers/Arm Warmers

What a great invention a leg warmer is. I've frankly never had much use for arm warmers, finding it far easier to slip on a jacket while still straddling my bike at a traffic light. But leg warmers allow you to ride in shorts far longer than you could otherwise (despite the second-skin feeling of Lycra tights, there's still no beating the springtime feel of pedaling in shorts when the days at last become warmer), because at that same traffic light I can reach over and blouse them down at my ankles or pull them up if it's turning cool.

Any leg warmer is better than none at all, but the kind with articulated knees (not just tubes, but shaped like a leg with a crook at the knee) and zippered sides near the foot are my favorites. The zipper allows you to pull them on without removing your shoes. (Many companies make Lycra leg warmers. Take a look at all of them, but be sure to check out Blackbottoms and Pearl Izumi. Both of these companies also make many other kinds of cycle clothes.)

▪ SOME FINAL THOUGHTS ON COMMUTING ▪

Let me say, before we end, that there are days when you should *not* commute on your bike. I've already mentioned the danger involved when snow builds up on shoulders, and when ice appears in treacherous invisible patches just waiting for the unsuspecting biker to lean into a turn. But it will be difficult to keep yourself from the challenge. I know, for I have the pleasure of recalling a Midwest winter when I missed not a single day of reaching work on time, on two wheels, in one piece. I had to leave once at three-thirty in the morning to make it to my first class on time, because the fifteen miles and ten inches of snow forced me to walk in places. And once, to the delight of my students, I made it to work sporting a fat lower lip—the result of failing to keep my bike upright on ice.

I was lucky. You might not be. So be a bit smarter and play it safe when the elements are at their worst. Meeting the challenge of bike commuting the rest of the year, and gaining the pleasure and physical fitness and saving money by doing so, should be satisfaction enough.

CHAPTER 5

TRAIL RIDING AND TOURING IN THE BACKCOUNTRY

If you're like most riders, it's only a matter of time before you'll hanker to take on a long all-day backcountry trail. Back at the trailhead at sundown you're satisfied, momentarily, and marvel during the drive back home at how far you went and how much fun it was.

And then the urge to do an overnighter strikes. You buy a rack, a pair of panniers and a bivy sack, and stay up half the night reading guidebooks and studying topos (topographic maps). And suddenly you're back at work on Monday morning locking your bike outside the office and telling everyone what a blast you had—and the places you plan to explore on a two-week jeep-roads-and-trail tour when vacation time rolls round.

Well, this chapter is designed to tell you how to go about it. There's no one correct way to tour. There are, however, a thousand bonehead things that we can do to make a tour less enjoyable. And I've done nearly all of them, since my first thin-tire tour in '65 and on hundreds of mountain bike tours since. I agree that learning by experience is best—but who says it has to be your *own* experience? I'll tell you what has worked for me, and at times what hasn't, and answer the questions I figure you might ask if we meet up at some trailhead.

Much of what you need to know is already present in other chapters, and later in the book you'll learn the repairs that will keep you from having to push your bike home. With the information here, plus a checklist to keep you from going off without a compass (literally), you'll be miles and miles ahead of where I was on my maiden voyage more than three decades of touring ago.

"Touring" for me, is spending a night (or more) out on the road or trail, the logical next-step progression from a long day ride where I'm forced to make it back to wherever I began. Short day rides are wonderful, of course, but they still prohibit us from leaving behind what we long to escape in the workaday world: *disciplined time.*

Multiday trips mean leisurely pedaling, hours and hours spent reconnoitering new territory with the knowledge that you've got all the next day (or more) to get back. Evening brings the simple making of a meal, and a final cup of java while the sun sets and the moon and stars rise. For me there's no better way to be restored to the "natural" pace of life.

Backcountry dirt-road and trail riding also offers us the experience of wheeled *and* boot explorations. Strap a small day pack over your rack and you can scramble to summits or explore woods or hollows or swamps at your pleasure. (I pull off the trail or road a bit, then hide my bike from view.) I find myself doing this more and more on my overnight tours, combining short hikes with long rides, so I'll discuss at length in this chapter the all-important element of footwear good for pedaling and hiking both.

I've passed nights on mountain bike tours trapped in my tent by a Colorado snowstorm at twelve thousand feet, and spent other nights in romantic Vermont bed-and-breakfasts after falling out of the Green Mountains. I have pedaled past cypress swamps in Louisiana and made my camps beneath Spanish moss–strewn water oaks, and on other rides marveled at Arizona's enormous two-ton saguaro cactus and awakened to a desert lizard on my chest. Mountain bikes, and a good pair of boots, offer you these touring experiences and a thousand others across this lovely land. Happy trails.

▪ CLOTHING ▪

Shorts

What you decide to pack when it comes to clothing depends entirely upon your expected length of travel and where you're headed. If you're on a multiday tour and will be stopping in small towns, you'll want clothes that are presentable in public. For me, that means a pair of non-Lycra shorts. Many of my riding partners wear their black Lycras into the backcountry and simply throw in a pair of hiking shorts to pull on over them in towns, but I prefer another approach. I don a pair of cycling briefs, made of a wicking polyester with the same padded suede insert that's present in regular cycling shorts (available through the Performance Bicycle mail-order catalog). I then pull on over them the most durable and rugged hiking shorts made, the Patagonia Stand-ups, which give me the pockets I like when hiking away from the bike and look good in town as well. (The Patagonia Baggies that I find so indestructible look too much like gym shorts for me to feel comfortable wearing them everywhere in public.)

If you're looking at sixty miles of pedaling, however, with no towns between, a pair or two of Lycras will do you. I don't care for the feel of these things while hiking away from the bike, and therefore pack a pair of regular briefs and Patagonia Baggies, which double perfectly as swimming trunks if the urge strikes.

Pants

Once again, life is made harder if your tour includes a town. Leg warmers do just fine when worn in conjunction with shorts for cool evenings around the camp. When it's cold, I add the rain pants over them. But walking around town dressed like that makes me feel dopey. In specialty catalogs there are some shorts with zippered legs, so that you have shorts and long pants both in the same package. But these are expensive, and while I haven't seen them up close I have to doubt, from the catalog description, that they'd hold up well to saddle abuse. My answer to this problem is to pack a very lightweight pair of hiking pants, full-cut so that walking and climbing in them is pleasurable. I've found that rolling these carefully, rather than folding them, produces fewer creases.

Shirt

I've never cared for the feel of bike jerseys, and think they look especially odd in the backcountry. The season will determine what you choose as clothing above the waist, but you should consider something long-sleeved (or the arm warmers I maligned earlier). If you're in the high country or anywhere in cooler seasons, a fleece sweatshirt or wool sweater could do double duty here.

Boots

For those who engage in more than one activity, if your checkbook and closet space can handle it, you could give Imelda a run for her money and fill your home and car with bike shoes, hiking boots, tennis shoes, running shoes, climbing shoes—the list boggles. And what if you engage in multiple activities away from your mobile closet (the automobile), like wanting to ditch your mountain bike for a two-mile rock scramble to a summit, or a day or two of hiking during a break from the saddle while on tour, or for that matter just a pleasant and painless stroll around town?

Specialization in the field of mountain bike shoes has not reached the point, thankfully, of our thin-tire racing and touring brethren. With most mountain bike shoes you can at least walk naturally when leaving the saddle. But I've yet to test a pair in which I'd be happy hiking for any distance, with or without a pack. The reason is, of course, that bikers must have relatively stiff shoes or their instep muscles take on the task of keeping the foot rigid on each downstroke of the pedals. And the harder you pedal (a result of heavy touring loads and tough terrain), the greater the strain if that support isn't present.

Hiking boots, on the other hand, needn't be this stiff, and are built more for lateral support (we only pedal forward, after all, while hiking is quite another matter). Plus we need tread to grip the trail. Too much tread, however, and we'd have a difficult time getting into and out of the toe clips. The perfect crossover boot is a very individual call.

I like the Clarion Impact Low, put out by Vasque, and like a million other hikers and bikers I've been on many a trail in this

Mountain biker donning hiking boots.

company's products. Of all the boots I've ever tested, these were by far the stiffest, yet are surprisingly comfortable when out of the saddle.

Make sure the shoe is extremely well padded and contoured inside to insulate the foot from the pedal shock that can occur after many miles, and cushion it over rocky terrain. They should be sturdy and breathable as well as relatively lightweight. Mine are two pounds five for the pair, not a light boot when compared to mountain bike cycling shoes in the bike shop, but comparable to other low-quarters designed with multisports in mind. The Vasque's toe-box is impregnated with a nylon-polyester mixture designed both to breathe and to retard moisture from entering; it also refuses

Vasque Clarion Impact Low

to be mashed down no matter how hard I strain up a hill—another feature to be on the look-out for. Vasque's polyester Sportee lining also fights wet feet by absorbing moisture and drying quickly. (*Always* purchase boots with removable, washable liners.) I've countered the problem of the Clarion's deep lugs that grip the trail like a knobby, but which *might* at first give you some difficulty in the clips by loosening my straps slightly, then accustoming myself to lift the foot a bit above the pedal when sliding in. To me, the extra insulation from the pedal and the great grip provided by these deep lugs is more than a fair trade-off. But you'll have to decide for yourself.

I hesitate to write about anything I've not tested personally, but Bill Skipper of Bend, Oregon, has been selling his PYRO Platform pedals (nine-inch-long injection-molded nylon platforms that replace a bike's pedals and screw into the crankarms in exactly the same way) to triathletes since April of '92.

Skipper will soon be offering a touring/mountain bike model with a guarded toe-piece, a couple of angled straps (that can be pulled tight or left somewhat loose, as I do when riding on both thin and mountain bike tires). They'll weigh 5½ ounces each, and you'll be able to pedal in anything you want—the wonderfully comfortable Air Mada Nikes, moccasins, flip-flops, or bare feet. (Address in the appendix, under the name VO2 MAX, Inc.)

And a few final comments. The very best place to buy boots is in a shop or store, where you can try them on, because true sizing is a problem and that can make mail-ordering them a pain. If you are intent upon catalog shopping, or cannot find the boots you want locally, be sure to order six weeks in advance of your trip. This will give you time to return a pair if necessary.

Also, wear the thickness of sock that you'll wear in the saddle and on the trail when you go to fit your boots. If these will be your winter boots as well bring a liner sock or a Gore-Tex sock with you.

And never, ever, leave for any trek in boots you've not used *doing exactly what you'll be doing in the wilds.* Boots that feel fine when worn around the house can change their spots when you add a pack and panniers.

Socks

Wickability. Cushioning. Durability. Temperature. These are the four qualities I keep in mind when purchasing trail socks. To start, scratch off any ideas of cotton socks (or socks with a high percentage of cotton). You'll get blisters, your feet will smell terrible in camp, and if they're "athletic" socks of a heavy cotton they'll take forever to dry out when you do your riding buddies a favor and wash the things.

I double sock it when I'm hauling heavy loads in winter on my bike, or tramping a lot of miles with a heavy backpack. My preference is usually an acrylic or polypropylene liner and a midweight acrylic or wool-blend on top. (Forget all-wool socks, even for winter. I've never had a pair that didn't wear a hole within a season.) Lots of socks add 10 to 15 percent nylon or stretch nylon to make them tougher, and some add a very small percentage of spandex as well. Don't buy socks according to your shoe size; they are (of course) measured differently. Choose a sock or sock combination that allows you sufficient room in your boots so your toes aren't squashed, and yet not so much wiggle room that blisters appear. If you do feel a blister coming on while out on the trail, stop *immediately* and apply moleskin, Spenco 2nd Skin, Compeed, or at last resort a small square of duct tape or a tire patch (no glue, please). A blister is a perfect site for infection, so you want to keep it from breaking open.

For my combination biking/hiking trips I find a single sock to be sufficient, unless it's winter and I'm donning another for warmth. My preference is the white Thorlo Running Crew in warm weather, and the Thorlo Trekking or Light Trekking sock when it's cool during the day and cold at night. In the coldest conditions I add the Thorlo Winter Liner. There are other good socks out there, but buy carefully and study the materials.

(See chapters 2 and 4 for gaiters, hats, gloves, etc.)

▪ SHELTER AND BEDDING ▪

Tents and Bivy Sacks

Begin searching for the perfect nighttime shelter in the wilds and you'll find that it's much like walking into the bike shop for the very first time: So many choices! One-person tents, two-person tents, tents to fit a group; three-season and four-season models; freestanding or pegged; bivy sacks for simple (and lighter) shelter—the list goes one. I'll attempt to make it understandable, but you should once again prepare yourself for a lengthy search.

You want a light weight tent that is stable and easy to assemble.

Naturally, you want a tent that is light, stable when erected, easy to put up and disassemble, of sufficient size, waterproof, and durable. As with bikes, unfortunately, such qualities come at a cost. Begin your search with an in-person, up-close look at some name-brand tents: Moss, North Face, Bibler, Sierra Designs are just a few. Compare the seams, stitching, fabrics, webbing, zippers, design, and poles with those of less expensive models. Give some thought to how much use you'll give it (it helps to think in terms of nights per year), and consider if long-term value makes the cost worthwhile.

Weight is always a critical factor with cyclists, of course, but especially so when contemplating a solo tour. (The load can be shared when there are more riders.) I'm speaking in the most general of terms, but for winter touring I try to keep my tent weight around four and a half pounds; for all other times, not much more than three. This would be relatively easy to accomplish if I weren't so completely sold on self-supported (freestanding) tents—those requiring no stakes to stand upright. The necessary cross-structure of poles on these tents increases their weight considerably. Self-supporters are much faster to erect, and, of course, they can be used *inside* other shelter, as I've done in unheated barns and large garages. Warming the relatively small airspace in my tent was far easier than making the larger areas cozy.

I buy what's called a three-season tent (with large screened areas for airflow), and just tough it out in winter. Four-season tents are heavier, and I don't like packing the extra weight. Besides, a good tent fly—a waterproof second wall against the elements, separate from and suspended just above the partially screened or mosquito-netted inner tent wall—keeps most of the wind away, and a good pad and sleeping bag see me through.

For summer desert travel I prefer almost completely screened tents. These are of course much lighter, but still heavy when compared to bivy sacks. The word "bivy" comes from "bivouac"—a temporary encampment in the open, with only tents or improvised shelter—and more specifically today refers to the close-fitting sacks that serve as bugproof, windproof, waterproof (depending upon the model you buy), extremely lightweight tents. Bivys have only a single wall (no rain fly), and I had never slept completely dry in one until the newest designs appeared, with full Gore-Tex tops and seam taping to keep out moisture that otherwise would work its way in through stitching holes. Nor had I ever been comfortable inside a burrito-style bivy until they began appearing with mosquito netting and circumferential poles to keep the bag off my face.

For summer camping in the desert, a screened tent comes in handy.

For the past year I've been using the Outdoor Research Advanced Bivy Sack, which has all these features and tips the scales at an ounce under two pounds. I've occasionally been unsure if a trail would require an overnight, and thus removed the poles and netting (cutting the weight down to twenty-two ounces) to pack what I consider my emergency shelter only. You don't have the luxury of roominess in a bivy, and I've missed that sorely on the two days of my life when pounding rains kept me inside mine, hunkered down with a book all day as well as night. But the weight savings over a tent makes a bivy the perfect shelter for biking/hiking backcountry trips. (There is an upside to cramped space: A bivy acts as a sleeping bag liner, actually raising—some companies claim by ten degrees—the comfort level of your bag.)

The size of your overnight shelter becomes a more important consideration when your tour is longer than a weekend. Pay attention to the actual measurements of whatever form of shelter you are considering. One bivy may be shorter and narrower than another, and all two-person tents are not the same size. As you did when choosing a bike, obtain catalogs and specification sheets for some deliberate, unrushed comparisons at home. Let me just add that for warm touring I now pack my bivy, but cold-weather rides of any length beyond a weekend make me choose my two-person tent, even when I'm riding solo. Why not save the weight and pack a one-person? Because of the extra gear I pack in cold weather, and because of the extra hours I'll be spending in the thing. The sun goes down early in winter, and rises late. And I'm inside many hours (once the cold has driven me from my campfire), reading by candlelight. At such times a little room, and a lot of comfort, makes the extra weight worthwhile.

A few suggestions: Needle holes in fabric allow moisture to follow the threads inside. Be sure, therefore, to seal your seams if they aren't taped. Some tents come with a tube of sealant; outdoor sporting goods stores and catalogs also carry it (Seam Seal is one such brand). A space blanket will serve as a ground sheet to protect your bivy or tent floor from rocks and twigs, but take a few minutes to clear the ground you've chosen for your bed. Also, forget about tarpaulins (tarps), the open-at-both-ends tents that hang from a rope suspended between two trees. Yes, the weight and dollar savings are great, but you get what you pay for. Rain and bugs fly in both ends, and putting up a tarp so that it won't flap about in the breeze is a real trick. (Tarps are great in an emergency, of course, but you'll be happier if you choose something more sophisticated for other times.)

Six inches of ripstop repair tape is good to have along, to prevent any fabric tears from becoming larger; always pack an extra tent stake or two as well. And put up your new tent at home before you take it out on the trails. Your first night's idyllic camp shouldn't be ruined by the realization that you're missing half the poles. (Note: If you've forgotten something and are in a pinch, be creative with what you do have. I've tied off my tent fly to my bike frame when nothing else was about, even used a spare spoke as a stake. And once, on the Colorado Trail, I watched with admiration while a buddy unplugged the gas line in his stove by separating one of the tiny metal strands from his brake cable.

Sleeping Bag

Skimp on most items for touring and you can, with a little greater effort, overcome the problems that result. But when the sun goes down and you crawl inside a crummy bag, all you can do is shiver.

The proper bag for a ride is therefore crucial. I carry a very lightweight semirectangular model for summer touring (comfort-rated at 45 degrees), and a modified mummy 0-degree heavyweight on winter rides. Now let's go over those terms.

Many riders at first think only in relation to temperature when it comes to bags. It's not a bad place to start, but don't stop there. Other considerations are:

Shape: (Rectangular, semirectangular, modified mummy, mummy.) The purpose of a sleeping bag is simply to trap your body heat, while keeping out the cold and at the same time allowing water vapor emitted by the body to escape.

A bag's shape is one of the critical elements in keeping the warmed air around you and cold air out. Rectangular bags are the most comfortable, resembling our beds at home, but of all the bag shapes they do the poorest job of retaining warm air and repelling cold, because it's impossible to pull the top of the bag around your neck and shoulders sufficiently. Your body must also work harder to warm the large air spaces created by that extra, comfortable shoulder, hip, and foot room.

A semirectangular bag is tapered toward the foot (reducing air space), yet still squared off at the top. On warm nights I can therefore adjust the amount of airflow for comfort; if there's a cold snap I can bundle up in clothing and still sleep pretty warmly.

A modified mummy is tapered at the foot and closer about the shoulders than is the semirectangular bag. In addition, the top is rounded to allow a close fit about the head—the spot from which we lose an amazing amount of body heat because of blood flow to the brain, face, and scalp. Full mummies, the warmest of shapes, are body-contoured throughout. But I find them far less comfortable for sleeping than are the modified mummies, because rolling over in them is difficult.

Early morning in the back country.

Fill: (Down or man-made insulation.) I would carry a down bag if I could be sure I could keep it dry (feathers mat when wet, providing almost *no* insulation; down also dries very, very slowly), if it were not so difficult to launder properly, and if the cost were more moderate. It has been written time and again that no man-made insulation is quite so compressible, quite so warm, or quite so good at maintaining loft (height of the insulating material in the bag).

But there have been great advances over the last two decades in man-made fills. Man-made materials are many, including Lamilite (the manufacturer Wiggy's proprietary synthetic, guaranteed *never* to lose loft), Hollofil, Quallofil, Primaloft, Polarguard, Thinsulate Lite Loft, Microloft. No matter what the fill, all bags feel horrible when they're wet. But man-made fills, unlike down, retain some 90 percent of their insulation when soaked, a critical difference in some situations that are not too difficult to imagine. They also dry out much, much more easily than down when the sun comes out the next day. Most man-made fills can also be machine-laundered and dried, without fears of clumping.

Loft: This refers to the height of the insulating material in the bag. The greater the loft, the greater the dead air space between you and the cold, thus providing increased warmth. You can help this by storing your bag properly, which means *not* leaving it crammed inside its stuff sack while at home. (You can also help it on the trail by fluffing out your bag as soon as you make camp, giving it time to regain maximum loft while you're making dinner and staring at the stars.) Several commercial products are available that guarantee improved loft if used when laundering a bag, but I've never tried them.

It should be obvious that a thicker bag is more comfortable, as well as warmer. Keep this in mind when assessing the importance of loft.

Construction: Features like offset quilting and shingled layers are much more critical for down, given its propensity for "cold spots." But since I prefer man-made fill, when I'm shopping for name-brand bags I pay more attention to loft and comfort rating, and assume the construction is fine.

However, no matter who the manufacturer is, I always look for what's called a zipper draft flap or insulated draft tube—a protective piece of insulation to prevent heat loss at the zipper junction. I also make sure the zipper has large tabs (or handles, to be found easily at night), that it does not bind or get caught easily in surrounding fabric when closed, is of good quality (if it looks cheesy it probably is), and doesn't unzip when there's movement of the bag (you don't want it unzipping every time you turn over during the night). For those of you who will be traveling with a partner, be sure to buy bags with right- or left-zipper openings, so that two bags can be zipped together for a warmer sleep and a more enjoyable camp. Finally, the draw cord (at the shoulders on a semirectangular, around the head on modified and mummy) should be placed conveniently, operate smoothly, and come equipped with an easily released lock.

Overall Weight: Don't get confused by "fill weights" when comparing bags. That term refers to just what it says—the weight of the insulation only. It's an important consideration, especially when comparing bags. But what you'll feel while pedaling is found in the "total weight" column.

My summer bag is light—barely over two pounds. My winter sack tips in at four pounds, eight ounces. That's heavy, making my shelter and bedding (counting ground pad) almost ten pounds by themselves. But when it's December, at night, in the cold, I don't begrudge an ounce.

I use a very old Quallofil summer bag, and a Wiggy's Lamilite for any time it might turn cool to freezing cold (I'm not alone in this choice; our Navy Seals, many search-and-rescue outfits, and the Canadian military also use Wiggy's). Also, the Wiggy's I purchased was a 20-degree bag, to which I add a liner from the same company that brings that comfort rating down to zero. (Slumberjack offers something along the same line with its Omni System series, in which two separate bags of two different comfort ratings zip together for coldest nights.) Last winter I tested a Cascade Designs bag in its Quantum line (comfort rated at 20 above, zero, and 20 below), and was impressed with the ergonomic foot box and the yoke storm collar. Remember, there's a bag out there that will keep you warm and comfortable no matter the conditions, *if* you choose carefully and if you keep it dry. If it doesn't come with a top-quality, completely enclosing, absolutely waterproof stuff sack, buy one.

Ground Pad

A good pad is a necessary part of your attempt to have a good, restful sleep. In cold weather it insulates your bag from the freezing, wet ground, and prohibits conductive heat loss (you should be heating the air in your sleeping bag and tent, not the earth). And at any time of year it's far more comfortable than sleeping in the dirt.

You'll find four kinds of pads when you start looking: air mattresses, closed-cell foam, open-cell foam, and self-inflating foam. Buy an air mattress if you're heading to the beach, and an open-cell foam pad if you want something comfortable in the back of the van (they damage too easily in the backcountry, insulate poorly, and act as a sponge when they meet up with moisture). Of the remaining two, you'll find the self-inflatable foam mattresses by far the more comfortable (I've used a Therm-A-Rest for years, just like millions of other bikers and hikers). The foam and air chamber are surrounded by a puncture-resistant nylon skin. Resistant as in *resistant*, not invulnerable. You've got to be good to these things or they won't work with you. I learned that lesson in Wyoming, when the highest five miles of the dirt jeep road a buddy and I were pedaling were covered with deep, sloshy snow. We attempted a crossing before sundown and didn't make it, so we camped around ten thousand feet and made a fire. Had I expected snow I'd have hauled along the small piece of an old closed-cell foam pad that I use as a seat in the wilds. Not wanting to sit in the wet, I pulled the inflated pad from my tent and perched high and dry. For about ten minutes. I'd made sure I was upwind of the fire and back far enough so that no cinders could blow upon my mattress and melt it. But I'd not made sure enough. The double moral here: Don't be as stupid as I was, and always carry the manufacturer's repair kit.

At about half the weight, and a quarter of the cost and comfort, closed-cell foam pads are in contrast almost indestructible. They also do a very good job of insulating the sleeper from the ground. I've used these things for years during warmer months (when it's *really* bitter I use one beneath my self-inflating foam mattress), and gotten by in the cold with them when I couldn't afford the weight on backpack or bike of the Therm-A-Rest. However, while I never have any trouble sleeping on one, you might—especially if you're a tosser-and-turner at home.

Cascade Designs, in an attempt to make closed-cell foam pads more comfortable, developed a Ridge-Rest with a series of ridges and valleys that also serve to trap your body's heat. The company's Z-Rest pad follows this design with what look like bubbles and depressions (I find this the most comfortable closed-cell I've ever used), and the thing folds up like an accordion, thus taking up less space than if rolled. I called company headquarters and questioned the durability of these fold-points when I first saw the pad, but was assured they'd been machine-folded and -unfolded thousands of times without a split. Which means far less to me than the fact that after three hard years of use in the field, mine still works like new.

Beyond construction, you must decide upon pad length. Regular length is about five feet, which for most of us means head or feet off one end. Long pads are about six feet in length, and thus insulate a body more fully from the ground. It seems an obvious choice, at least in cold weather. But that extra foot of pad can add a third to half a pound. I pack a short one in warm weather, a long one in cold.

A pillow? I don't know about you, but I have a difficult time sleeping without one. I used to make one by stuffing clothing inside whichever stuff sack was empty at the moment, but it forced me to accustom my head to a different shape each night. It's a lot of extra weight, but if you can drop the bucks and handle an extra 1½ ounces, Cascade Designs offers a fifteen- by twenty-inch Pocket Pillow into which you stuff your parka or other clothes. (Other companies sell similar pillow sacks.) The consistency might still be different each night, but at least the shape will be the same.

▪ COOKING ON THE TOUR ▪

Many thin-tire tourers, looking to save on weight and usually not more than a couple of hours from a store or café, decide against packing a stove. I do

Peanut butter and jelly is the staple of most backcountry cyclist.

quite well on most paved tours with my always-in-the-pannier complement of peanut butter, bread, jam, and cheese, supplemented daily by store purchases of fresh fruit, vegetables, more cookies than I care to admit, and trips to local cafés.

But things are different in the backcountry. When you are planning rides away from towns for days and days you'll want to add the weight of a stove to your gear.

Stoves

The three factors when one considers a stove are type of fuel, weight, and cost. In the first of these categories the choice is among butane, white gas (Coleman or similar brands), kerosene, alcohol, and multifuel (some of which will burn all the above but butane, plus auto gas and even jet fuel; this does not mean, however, that they burn all fuels equally well). Yes, I've left out propane, but that's because I've yet to see a propane bottle I'd be willing to pack on a bike. And of course there are pros and cons with all the fuels you might haul along.

Butane is by far the most convenient. It comes in canisters that are simply plugged into the stove and fired up—no priming or pumping required. Disadvantages are the extreme high cost compared to, say, white gas (roughly ten times more expensive), limited availability, the need to keep the canisters warm in winter (I put one in my sleeping bag at night—wrapped in a T-shirt, of course), and the fact that they must be packed out even when empty and still aren't recyclable.

White-gas stoves, in contrast to butane, must be pumped. This is an extremely minor chore, as is the preheating sometimes necessary in cold weather. These stoves boil water faster than does butane; fuel is plentiful and inexpensive throughout the United States and Canada but less so overseas.

Kerosene stoves, on the other hand, will not find fuel wanting anywhere, and it's inexpensive. But it smokes upon lighting, it's oily (spills don't evaporate quickly), it can be difficult to light, and the smell is terrible. Alcohol as a fuel puts out only half as much heat as does white gas, it's more expensive, and it can be difficult to find.

The three stoves I've used most often in the backcountry are the MSR Whisperlite (which uses an external bottle of white gas, and is well loved by many for its simplicity and durability), the Hank Roberts (to which must be attached a butane bottle), and the Coleman Peak 1 (both the white-gas-only model and the multifuel, both of which have a convenient fuel storage tank directly beneath a burner; the multifuel model is a full one-third lighter than the white-gas-only Peak 1). Most often I find myself packing the Hank Roberts and a single butane cartridge if one of the other riders has offered to cook; I pack mine just so I can make coffee for the gang. I alternate between my Whisperlite and Coleman Peak 1 the rest of the time, when I need hot fires and assured availability of fuel.

As for cooking gear, I do all gourmeting in a single pot (with lid), and employ only a gripper and a set of sturdy Lexan plastic utensils. (I should warn you that I might not be the best example; I cook with scarcely more at home.) I pack half a kitchen sponge/scrubber for washing up, plus biodegradable soap. And last, though you'll encounter the warning in the stove's instructions I'll add it here: Do not operate any model stove inside a closed tent or too close to a tent wall or roof. Not only might you have to reshingle when the flame flares unpredictably, but also you might not live to do so. Carbon monoxide is a by-product with every stove; good ventilation is a must.

Food

Meals in the backwoods are similar whether you're backpacking or touring, although you can carry more weight on a bike than you can on foot. For dinner, I boil a couple of cups of water, throw in two handfuls of precooked Minute Rice, or cous-cous, sprinkle half a box of Knorr's soup and some jerky into the concoction, and roughly five minutes later am chowing down. I vary the taste with different kinds of Knorr's soup, and occasionally opt for a Lipton or other-brand pasta bag, the kind that tells you to add $1\frac{1}{2}$ cups of water and a half cup of milk, then boil for eight to ten minutes. I find these taste just fine without the milk, and so save the powdered white stuff for my granola at breakfast. Both my standard trail dinners are filling (important in cold weather for sleeping warm, since your body needs the fuel to keep things heated), they cook in a single pot (out of which I eat), and require minimal cleanup.

Breakfast in warm seasons is usually granola, over which I sprinkle powdered milk, add water, and stir. The stove if present is cranked up for coffee, and in cold weather for hot instant oats drowned in honey.

Which leaves only lunch, and the twenty or so snack breaks between sunup and when I blow out my candle lantern. Midday meals are always

Instant oatmeal doused in honey makes a great breakfast on cold mornings.

uncooked, unless it's been a wet and sloppy ride and suddenly I've spied a dry, inviting rock overhang or cave. But usually it's peanut butter (which I never eat at home, by the way), jam, bread, and cheese, or sage rubbed between the hands and sprinkled over the peanut butter if the jam is gone and I'm out west. Snacks are anything I happened to have a fancy for the last day before the ride, and threw liberally into a pannier. But almost always this includes great quantities of dried fruit, jerky, and energy bars.

So much for the cooking detail. Some additional tips: (1) Pack your peanut butter and jam, and especially the honey, in high-quality, plastic, screw-lid jars. I've never met a snap-lock lid that can handle a rough bike trail, and panniers are never quite the same inside once coated with honey and jam. You'll have trouble forever with critters as well, big ones like bears or perhaps as small as the raccoon that once ate through my partner's handlebar bag to get at our Italian sausage. (2) You'll save yourself a lot of money in the long run if you, and perhaps some biking/hiking friends, invest in a dehydrator. They're great for deer, elk, beef, even chicken jerky, and will expand your menu of dried fruits far beyond that offered by even the best-stocked health stores. (3) Do *not* keep food, or even clothes impregnated with the smell of food, in your tent overnight when you're in bear country. Pack a shank of parachute cord or very lightweight rope and suspend these items in a sack at least ten feet off the ground and away from your campsite.

■ MISCELLANEOUS REQUIREMENTS ■

The following items have not always been with me in the backcountry, but when they weren't they were sorely missed. This now makes them requirements for me; they might be for you. Think carefully before you decide against tossing them into your saddlebags.

Light

There's nothing handier than a headlamp for erecting a tent or repairing your bike once the sun's gone down. It frees up both hands and follows your eye direction. I've owned the Recreational Equipment Incorporated (REI) big-lens plastic type that you pull forward to turn on and slap yourself in the forehead to switch off. I've also had the simple strap-and-loops kind that holds a Mini Mag light on the side of the head. Petzl, the company to which many cavers owe their skins, makes some beautifully engineered small-to-large forehead lights whose rotary switches will not turn on by themselves while jostling around in your panniers. (I use two strong rubber bands to hold my REI pull-on light in the off position.)

So, you've got a lot of choices, including numbers and types of batteries, battery placement, and replacement bulb. I choose lights that employ two double A's (the same kind used by the photo equipment I haul with me on every backcountry ride), that have the batteries in the lens compartment (no external waist-mounted battery pack and wire running up your back), and that have a spare bulb tucked away somewhere inside the headlamp unit itself.

For rides requiring only one or two nights out I pack a headlamp only, plus two extra batteries for reading time. On longer rides, however, I take the brass candle lantern I bought on tour in Santa Fe back in the early '80s, and have used countless nights in the wild. This simple metal/glass globe lantern is the best system yet invented for reading in a tent. Dripless candles burn brightly (and impart a surprising amount of heat in a small space) for eight or nine hours, and the lantern itself weighs only five ounces in aluminum—which is the kind I used when efficiency meant more to me than the beauty of the slightly heavier brass lantern I bought on that ride through New Mexico.

When I'm on extended tours in regions I fear will have no replacement candles, buddies send them to me—general delivery, with the package clearly marked HOLD FOR PICKUP—at post offices along the way. Have the packages marked in that manner or they'll be returned after ten days. And if your route changes or you lose your way, you can always drop a line to the post office superintendent requesting that he return the package.

Compass

Despite my map-reading classes in the Army and all the time I've spent in the field, I'm still lousy at orienteering with topos and a compass. But when the single trail or jeep road I'm following hits a junction offering me three directions of travel, I can, with my compass, figure out which to take. Anything you have that points north, even a lodestone or dime-store com-

Compass with topo map.

pass, is better than nothing, but a good compass built for backcountry use and abuse will be willing to work when you need it. I've needed the mirror-and-fold-down-cover Brunton model I carry many times, when too many roads and trails forked off and when I couldn't see *any* in a sudden white-out and had to find my path. Also, because I like to ditch my bike and hike, often cross-country, I prefer a mirror sighting line when I determine my line of travel. The compass appealed to me because it came in a small nylon carrying case that also enclosed notes on making a solar still, ground–air emergency code markings, some first-aid tips, and a tiny ($2\frac{1}{2}$- by $5\frac{1}{2}$-inch) book on compass skills. It's comforting to know that when you can't count on your brain, a book is around to help out. The whole package weighs in at four ounces.

Water Purification

Known for some time as the backpacker's bane, *giardia lamblia*—a water-borne parasite that begins its life cycle when swallowed, and one to four weeks later has its host bloated, vomiting, shivering with chills, and living in the bathroom—unfortunately attacks backcountry bikers as well. Discovered by Anton van Leeuwenhoek in 1681, the disease is known by most today simply as giardia, and is avoided by boiling water, the addition of tetraglycine hydroperiodide tablets (sold under the far easier names of Potable Aqua, Globaline, Polar Pure, Emergency Germicidal, and Coughlan's), or by filtration through a water purifier. (The tablets impart a mild iodine taste to the water, but this can be eliminated with Potable Aqua's P.A. Plus neutralizing tablets.)

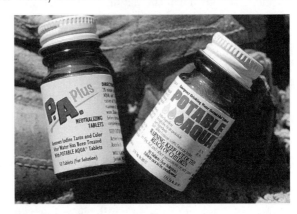

All water in the backcountry, even if it's crystal clear and free-flowing in a mountaintop stream, should be treated. Don't think that just because you're above the elevation of sheep and cattle summer grazing lands that

Water purification tablets.

Filters allow you to drink water without having to boil it first.

you're out of danger; wild and domestic animals both can pass giardia. I've had good success with pump filters, which I like for their fast action and the ability to drink the water immediately. What I don't like is the weight and bulk of the things, and the fear of breakdown (their filters become clogged; always pack a spare). I now therefore use tablets exclusively, always waiting the prescribed twenty minutes after treatment and making sure, if I'm with a group and water purification is my assigned task, that no rider is pregnant or has a thyroid condition. Pills are cumbersome and time-consuming when you're with a group, and someone usually caves in and brings along a pump. But there's absolutely nothing better on a solo tour.

Trowel

Often sold as the "backpacker's shovel," this is a necessity for burying human waste. Which is something you've got to do, and do properly, not just hide it beneath a mess of leaves like most hunters. Dig a cathole (nine or so inches deep), burn the paper, then cover all with dirt and tramp down. This bury-and-burn technique is little trouble for the health and aesthetic benefit. Animals will sometimes dig up wastes, and thus expose unburned paper to dry in the sun and blow about the forest or woods. Be sure that the paper is burned out completely and all fire is extinguished before you cover with dirt.

Signal Mirror

These are great little inventions, especially for solo backcountry bikers who in their wildest dreams figure they might someday wind up snakebit and too bloated to pedal, or with a broken leg. Any mirror will work to signal other people you happen to spy on a hillside or in a valley too far off to hear your yells, but try to aim a reflection at a passing plane and I can guarantee that you'll be off by *critical* degrees.

My signal mirror weighs half an ounce, cost a pittance, and is a champ at directing its eye-blinding spot of light. It has a hole in the middle of the mirror through which you locate the reflection on a tree or rock, then you slowly raise it to the passing plane and hope somebody's looking. It has directions on the back and works even in hazy conditions. (This item, as well as most backcountry travel and survival gear, can be found at your local REI store or call for an REI or Campmor catalog; numbers in the appendix.)

Whistle

A whistle is used to signal for others in case of an emergency. If you ride solo it's especially useful; the sound of your whistle will be far more audible than your voice to a passing hunter.

Madden Mountaineering's Off-Road Kit

What happens when the long one-day bike ride unexpectedly becomes an overnighter? And because you didn't want to pack a lot of needless weight you left all but tools and a few Power Bars back home? Well, I know the answer because I've done it, as have most other boneheads once in their lives. You pass a miserable, freezing night of no sleep, trying your best to recall all those easy Boy Scout methods of making a fire in the rain, and contemplating the taste of oak leaves.

The Off-Road Kit is a great eight-ounce insurance policy against this happening to you, and is perfect as a carry-always for day-riders who won't be hauling all the other gear I mention. You'll need to add some water purification tablets and a few energy bars, but that's it. The kit includes:

1 dermiclear tape
2 gauze pads
4 aspirin tablets
3 adhesive bandages
2 polysporin ointment packets
1 providone iodine towelette
1 razor blade

1 safety pin
24-inch wire
36-inch duct tape
15-foot nylon cord
1 fire starter flare stick
1 box waterproof matches
1 high-intensity whistle
emergency note cards and instructions
tube tent/tarp
dextrose cubes

▪ LOADING A MOUNTAIN BIKE ▪

If you're loading up for just one or two nights, and if your tour isn't in winter, you should have no difficulty in bike handling once you've strapped your sleeping bag, tent or bivy, and ground pad to the back rack (I bungee my day

A fully loaded bike

pack over the top of these when I plan to do some hiking), and stowed all your other gear and food inside your panniers. You'll have to be thoughtful of your rear spokes in your riding style, however, due to the additional strain they always endure when compared to front wheel spokes.

Where mountain bikers really begin noticing differences in handling is when longer tours and inclement weather require so much weight that some must be shifted up front. Because it's preferable to have as much weight as possible on a bike packed low and close to the frame, choose a front rack and small panniers over a humongous handlebar bag. If my ride is primarily on jeep or Forest Service roads, I pack according to the rules we use on thin-tire bikes: one-third total weight up front, two-thirds in the rear. If I've got a lot of *rough* jeep-road riding ahead of me (which is often the case at the steepest climbs, where the road is chewed up by jeep tires), or single- or double-track trail riding as well as road, I attempt to shave a bit more of the weight from the front to the rear (closer to a one-quarter/ three-quarter proportion). The reason is that hopping any obstacle, or any other kind of creative steering, is difficult with much weight up front.

Road riding is wonderful aerobic exercise, and really gets the leg muscles in shape. But mountain biking—especially mountain bike touring— works out the upstairs muscles as well. Be prepared for this if you aren't already doing full-body workouts at home; you're going to be one sore puppy in your arms, back, and neck come day three. But you'll be a much stronger human overall once you've done more of it.

And now for some specific "gear location" and other tips:

1. I've told you before how sold I am on CycoActive's BarMap OTG, the Cordura-and-clear-vinyl map holder that rides folded up and attached to the handlebars, but unfolds to show a full 8½ by 11 inches of whichever map you're using (it will hold a map as large as 25 by 44 inches). Well, in its pockets I carry my compass and (at times) my snakebite kit, knowing I'll need the one often, and if I ever need the other, I'll want it in a hurry.

2. Purchase an under-the-saddle bag large enough to hold at least your poncho, the first item you'll want to don when there's a storm. If possible, keep your chaps and saddle cover (if you pack one) there as well. Next in rainwear, I house all my pannier covers in a single bag, preferably along with my rain boots. This way there is but a single zipper to work, not four or five. Seconds count when attempting to

keep dry, plus this way you're opening only one bag to the drops. And don't forget to seam-seal your pannier covers.

3. Tent, sleeping bag, and ground pad for me always ride perpendicular to and on the rear rack. As the tent is usually the heaviest of these items, it rides forward of the sleeping bag on the rack; the ground pad rests on top, between the two. On long backcountry treks I pack a spare tire, which I fold into an "O," duct tape in place, then bungee to the top of my front rack. And on top of this sit my vest and parka in a stuff sack, allowing me easy access without having to go into or take up the space in a pannier.

4. Regular sandwich bread is enough of a pain to keep from smashing on thin-tire tours; it's next to impossible to keep from mangling on an ATB. The flat pocket bread is a good alternative, and bagels are great too. Also, get in the habit of packing food on the derailleur side of the bike; it won't get smashed when you lay your bike down— always, loaded or not—on the *non*-derailleur side.

5. As suggested earlier, carry peanut butter, jam, honey, and any similar items in high-quality, screw-lid plastic jars. Also, pack all fresh fruit in plastic bags. Even the hardest pear will develop bruises after the first few miles; after ten it will get revenge by smearing itself all over your bike bag.

6. Fail to follow my (1–5) suggestions and the result will be a nuisance. But *this* can be critical: Large items carried outside the panniers (and therefore unprotected by waterproof bag covers) must be in absolutely waterproof stuff sacks. On midwinter tours I even double-sack my sleeping bag, just to be sure. You'll shudder when you see how much a good stuff sack costs, but get these items soaked in cold weather, or in high summer when you're in the desert or mountains, and you'll wish you'd spent the bucks. And as you do with other seams you want not to leak, use seam seal on all stuff sacks.

■ PANNIERS ■

The advances in pannier design are amazing. Even the worst bag made today is far better than what "worked" in the distant past, and there are now many lines of bags developed specifically for mountain bikes, engineered to handle the shock and abuse of off-road travel. They're beautiful to the eye, easy to mount, stable on the bike, quickly and easily opened, and durable. But without exception they aren't cheap. Know this before you begin your search, and know also that there's no reason that they should be. I've stood next to bag builders in three different states, watching as expensive materials and state-of-the-art hardware were formed, stitched, and restitched into the shape of a pannier. The process is time-consuming and difficult, as a close inspection of any well-built bag will show.

All this good news about great bags means once again you are faced with a host of wonderful choices. As I suggested in chapter 1 concerning buying your bike, determine your need (commuting and short overnights or weeklong tours?), decide what you can spend, make an extremely thorough search of the market, then make your purchase and have a blast.

Here are some notes that should help prepare you for what you'll find on hangtags and in catalogs.

Materials

Most panniers are constructed of various weights of Cordura nylon. Many sport a urethane coating to enhance water resistance, but as mentioned before, nothing protects your bag and its contents in a downpour as well as a raincover. (Be sure the cover has an opening of some kind at the bottom—most use a simple grommet—or water will collect there in a pool and soak the base of the bag.) Polyester thread, designed not to stretch, mildew, shrink, or break down due to ultraviolet radiation, is sometimes employed at eight to ten stitches per inch (with double- and even triple-stitching at stress points). I check to see that the stitching is uniform, not sloppy, though the pride involved and the quality control of most bag builders are such that very few flaws make it out of the factories.

Large, heavy-duty, self-repairing zippers (with wide zipper coverings to ward off raindrops), tough nylon and polypropylene webbing, steel or tempered aluminum hardware, and metal or poly unbreakable stiffeners (be *sure* they're unbreakable) are some of the offerings and materials that you'll see trumpeted in pannier catalogs. It might sound like so much blather now, but these things count out on the trail.

Construction

Some panniers are, in design, a rather simple sack. Others sport a number of outside zippered Cordura pockets, external zippered (or open) mesh pockets (most often used for drying clothes), lashtabs (to which one can lash equipment with optional webbing), snaps for mating with another pannier, compression straps (to hold the weight close to the frame), and top-of-the-bag web handles to make carrying easier when the packs are off the bike. (See the photos of Robert Beckman Designs panniers for an excellent bag with internal pockets.)

Thin-tire packs are often large and very often rectangular; this shape helps them to sit upright when off the bike, and of course allows greater volume than does a rounded-bottom bag. If you are considering one of the larger pannier sets today and your mountain bike has very short chainstays (or normal stays but your feet are size fifteen or so), you should determine if the heel of each foot is going to strike the bag on the upstroke.

Be sure your panniers are securely attached to your bike before loading up.

Attachment

Thin-tire riders can get by with simple hook-and-spring (or elastic band) mounting systems, counting on gravity to keep the hooks (located at the top of the bags) in place and the bottom spring or band to hold the base of the bag next to the frame. It doesn't work that way off-road.

Back in the late '80s I had the displeasure of stopping many times during a four-day, four-mountain-pass, jeep-roads tour while my five riding partners collected their panniers. My on-road/off-road Needleworks bags (the former name of Robert Beckman Designs bags) never budged, of course, due to their deathlike grip onto Bruce Gordon racks. Nor did the Madden packs pop off, thanks to their simple strap-and-buckle backup to the hook-and-band mounting system. But all the rest went flying.

Since then I've tested many attachment systems, all of which sounded simple and foolproof

Packing all your touring gear in a trailer pulled behind the bike—instead of cramming it into panniers and on top of luggage racks—is hardly a new idea. What *is* new is a trailer that allows you to pedal narrow single-track trails and bump along creek bottoms. Meet the B.O.B. (Beast of Burden)—a 12-pound, 17-inch wide, single-wheeled trailer that will follow you almost anywhere you can steer a bike, even a full-suspension-frame. The perforated chro-moly steel cargo bed is sturdy and low to the ground (creating little wind resistance); a huge duffel bag holds all the gear you'd otherwise have hanging on your frame. The trailer's front fork attaches easily to the bike's rear axle, which means you can detach it quickly once you're in camp and pedal nearby trails with an unencumbered mount. Just as with panniers it takes time to get used to the load, and you'll have to remember, once you've successfully negotiated a light turn or narrow passage with your bike, the trailer must still make it through as well.

on paper, but many of which proved impractical for the road, much less the trail. One company, for a while, offered a "lever-lok" whose crucial rubber compression pad jiggled loose on single-track. Others, then and currently, have systems that require involved behind-the-bag adjustments, or straps that must be handled or pulled in this way or that. When you're holding the pannier in the bike shop, back-side up and in full view, or when you see it displayed like this in a photo or drawing in a catalog, it seems a simple task to perform. But it might well be a different story when the bag is hanging on a rack, with the strap or lever or whatever needs attending in the dark and out of sight. Is it in such a place on the bag that it's easy to reach? Can it be reached by someone with hands your size? (My hands are somewhat large; I've had trouble with teacup-sized loops and hooks in the past, and curse the things when it's cold and wet and I'm forced to remove overgloves to work them.)

Finally, even if it works, is the attachment or detachment system cumbersome? Compare it to a Madden, a Robert Beckman Designs, or a Lone Peak, three systems (and there are more) that can be operated even by those with the manual dexterity of ungulates. Is it time-consuming? If so, don't listen to the salesperson who says you'll almost never be taking them off during a tour anyway. Yes, it will stay on the bike if you're camped out and the bike's by the tent. But in drumming rain and heavy snow I take mine off to put them in the tent or vestibule. When I'm traveling through towns I often remove a bag to haul along with me, and when I occasionally grab a motel or bed-and-breakfast I strip the bike and ride it about unloaded.

Content Accessibility

This is a very important factor with me, as I'm in and out of my panniers many times during the day. Because of this I prefer the contents to be only a zipper opening away, not some involved process of multiple side-release buckles and drawstrings. Also because of my desire for easy access I prefer a front-loading bag, one in which the zipper runs down either side far enough to expose the contents to view. Top-loading bags present one with the task of trying to see and reach past the top layer of contents to access what's below.

If you're a backpacker you already know this argument, and have heard opposing testimony. Ultimately, it's your choice.

▪ UNLOADED TOURING ▪

Sounds great, doesn't it, after all the "heavy" talk above? By far the majority of all-terrain tourers seem to prefer it, packing only tools and a change of shorts and a couple of credit cards. Riding unburdened toward a warm shower, white tablecloths, and clean sheets just can't be beat. I love to do it occasionally, both for the sheer hedonistic pleasure and for the stark contrast that it provides to all my other touring. Before you fall into the "either/or" school of tourers, however, give yourself a taste of each.

For the moment, let's say you plan to ride "unloaded" over trails and Forest Service roads to a confirmed motel reservation in some backwater town. First ask yourself some questions: What's the safe minimum of gear to carry? What if there's a bike breakdown or accident? What if there's a storm? You'll never be able to pack what you'd need to rebuild your whole bike. But what about the common problems of flats? A broken gear or brake cable?

So you know you need tools, replacement parts, and some know-how (see chapter 7). Beyond this, I suggest you pack the very minimum of what the season might require for you to survive the night out on the trail. Not "spend it comfortably"—then you'd be hauling all the stuff you'd take if you didn't have reservations. Just the minimum required to get you by without giving up the ghost—or being so miserable that you'd be willing to. At least take The Off-Road Kit by Madden Mountaineering. You'll have the tube tent that's inside, plus the fire starter, and there's even a razor blade should you decide it's all a bit too much. I pack my bivy, a pair of long underwear, and a stocking cap. You'll be amazed at how much warmer you sleep in the cap. And you'll probably be so happy to see morning that you won't even mind that it's the start of a very bad hair day.

▪ BACKCOUNTRY MAPS ▪

Unloaded touring and long one-day rides require that you have a good idea of how much ground can be covered in a day. Being realistic about the num-

Cyclists consulting over a map.

ber of miles you can cover during the number of hours available is one element in determining that distance. A second factor is a recent and, it is hoped, accurate weather report. A third factor is the condition (as far as you know it) of the trail or road you'll be following. There is a fourth element as well to consider, every bit as important and perhaps more so than all the rest—terrain.

Fortunately, there are maps that provide both the distance between two geographic points and the elevation variation between. These are called topographic, or "topo" maps (pronounced with both vowels long), issued by the Department of the Interior United States Geological Survey National Mapping Division—referred to simply as the USGS.

The elevation gain and loss in a topo are indicated through the use of contour lines, squiggly lines that spread out across the map like an ill-formed spiderweb. At the bottom of each map is a contour interval designation of so many feet. Large-scale, single-state maps (1:500,000 scale; one inch equals eight miles), for instance, have a contour interval of five hundred feet. This means that every time a contour line is encountered along the route you'll be traveling, you'll be gaining or losing five hundred feet of elevation. Occasional figures written on these lines tell you whether you will be pedaling up or down those five hundred feet. Now, if half a dozen of these lines exist in close proximity, you know you're pulling a mountain pass—or zooming down one. And if your path is free of these lines you're pedaling the plains, or struggling up and down a lot of 499-foot hills that don't show up on this large-scale a map. For this reason, state-scale topos are usually left to our thin-tire brethren.

The next scale of topos is the 1:250,000, in which one inch equals four miles and the contour interval is two hundred feet. I find these and the full-state maps of interest in determining what piece of a major geological formation I will be traveling, like the Southwest's Colorado Plateau, or Vermont's Green Mountains, or the Ouachita Range of Arkansas. But the contour interval still allows too many high hills to elude detection, and thus helps me very little in determining how long it might take to cover my intended route.

Better by far is the 1:62,500 scale, in which one inch equals one mile and the contour interval is eighty feet. But best of all is the 1:24,000 scale (more popularly known as the "7.5-minute" series, but pronounced *seven-and-a-half*). In these detailed beauties, one inch along your trail equals two thousand feet of linear pedaling, and every contour interval represents forty feet of elevation. Now *that's* a map.

Okay, counting contour lines is easy, as is checking the numbers on them to see if you're heading up or down. But getting a good idea of your total distance between two points is made more problematic by the detail. After all, how can you lay your ruler alongside all those twists and turns in your intended trail? The answer—a planimeter (accent on the second syllable). Also called a map measurer, the planimeter has a tiny metal wheel that you roll along the map; a needle and gauge compute the inches traveled.

Topographic maps also provide detailed road classifications. Different colorings or markings indicate the categories of interstate, heavy-duty, medium-duty, light-duty, unimproved dirt roads, and jeep trails. They are, in other words, great if you're on any kind of road. Map symbols include everything from footbridges and overpasses to dams and canals. Various shadings indicate swamps, wooded marshes, vineyards, orchards, and more. And if your route takes you to a glacier, your topo will show you the best way around it.

But this detail comes at a cost—that of so many maps being required for relatively short rides. On my 107-mile dirt-road ride along the Lolo Trail, for instance, following Lewis and Clark's route (and the 1877 Nez Percé retreat) across Idaho's Bitterroot Mountains, I needed thirteen 7.5-minute maps to cover the distance. Not wanting to ruin my investment in these maps while on the ride, I photocopied the portions of the maps that covered my route and left the originals at home.

If your route takes you through a national forest, you'll have the very great pleasure of plotting your progress on maps issued by the National Forest Service. These are of a larger scale than the 7.5-minute topos (1/2 inch equals one mile; my Lolo Trail route that required thirteen 7.5-minute topos was covered by a single Forest Service map; unlike topos, they are printed on front and back both). Forest Service maps are covered by a grid that is helpful in determining distances and contain not just roads but trails as well, *but* they do not provide topographic information.

An important bit of information that is present in both USGS and Forest Service maps is the year when the map data reflected was gathered. The map you're counting on for navigation and that you purchased just the day before might be current, and it might be fifteen years old. So keep your wits about you in the wilds. If you aren't pedaling a popular and populated (with other riders) and well-marked trail, take your compass, all the pertinent maps, and the minimum emergency items I've suggested. Remember: Your safety in the backcountry is first and foremost *your* responsibility.

Don't count on someone else picking up the slack.

A third set of maps of great use to mountain bikers who are pedaling through areas well traveled by bikers, hikers, and backcountry skiers is put out by Trails Illustrated. Unlike the paper government maps that must be treated (Campmor catalog offers Map Seal waterproofing), these are waterproof and tearproof, and their cost reflects it. Before you shy away from dropping the extra dollars, however, let me add that all Trails Illustrated maps are revised every one to three years. They have both the trails information of a Forest Service map and topographic contour lines, sometimes larger scale inset maps, route summaries and other helpful tips, addresses, and phone numbers. They are sold at many outdoor sport shops and bookstores, and are in my estimation the single best source of map-only information for mountain bikers.

Sources for these maps if you've scoured the appropriate stores in your town and come up empty are as follows:

Locating USGS Maps

First, look in the white pages of your phone book under the U.S. Government listings, find the Department of the Interior heading, and run your finger hopefully down the entries until USGS Office pops out. Give them a buzz and ask when they're open to sell maps to the public. Or write to the following address, ask for an index, plus a price list and a copy of the booklet *Topographic Maps*. This will help you to read them in the field.

USGS Map Sales
Box 25286
Denver, CO 80225

Locating Forest Service Maps

Look in the white pages of your phone book under the U.S. Government listings, find the Department of Agriculture heading, and hope you next see the words "Forest Service" beneath it. If so, give them a call and they'll provide the address of the regional Forest Service office, from which you can obtain the appropriate map. If not, ask directory assistance to locate the number of the Forest Service district office that administers whichever national forest it is you'll be traveling through. Call that office and request your map.

Locating Trails Illustrated Maps

Call their office at 800-962-1643, or write to them at:

Trails Illustrated
P.O. Box 3610
Evergreen, CO 80439

They will inform you if they have a map of the region you plan to pedal, and upon request will also send a free catalog of their many maps.

Other Trail Information Sources

If there's a ranger or superintendent of the land you frequently pedal, be it Bureau of Land Management (BLM) or county park or whatever, ask if there's a map available for mountain bikers. Chances are good you aren't the first to ask, and chances are even better that some of the landkeepers are mountain bikers themselves. I've often followed routes from photo-copied hand-drawn maps, and learned of trails not to miss and those to avoid not from rangers looking askance at my bike but from friendly, smiling fellow bikers in their day-job uniforms.

Bike shops, of course, are the expected repositories of regional trail information, and should be the first place you stop when you visit an area with which you're unfamiliar. The salespeople and mechanics might be too busy with customers to give you directions, but most will have for sale any existing books for maps on area trails, and many will have photocopies of hand-drawn maps or USGS maps taped to a wall with routes highlighted.

There is no better source of trail info than a fellow cyclist who has pedaled it. Which brings us to bikers' guidebooks and guide maps, the next best thing to having that person pedaling just beyond your front wheel. I mentioned bike shops as one place to look for such information. Another is *The Cyclists' Yellow Pages,* an annual "directory for bicycle trip planning" put out by the Adventure Cycling Association (formerly old Bikecentennial). They're a wonderful bunch of committed people who are currently developing The Great Divide Mountain Bike Route, which when completed will with detailed maps guide you through the Rockies clear from Canada to Mexico.

You can ask what's available and order any book or map by calling 800-721-8719 (Monday–Friday, mountain time). You can join the organization, by writing or calling them (see the appendix for that number and address) at a respectable time of day. And on top of feeling and doing good you'll get a great monthly magazine.

The League of American Bicyclists (formerly The League of American Wheelmen) is an excellent organization that's been lobbying for cyclists' rights since 1880, and like the association above sends out a great monthly magazine and thick annual compendiums (the *Almanac* and *Tourfinder*) of all kinds of information of importance to riders. State-by-state listings of local LAB-chapter officers and bike touring directors, plus publications and maps and notable annual cycling events are just some of what you'll find in their publications. Both these organizations, by the way, offer "bikes-fly-free" policies when you join up and use one of their "partner airlines." If you fly with your bike one time a year, and in just *one* direction, you'll save more than the cost of the annual membership. LAB also offers a Hospitality Homes Network, in which free lodging with fellow bikers across the nation is possible. (Address and phone in appendix.)

The third group to lead me from my solitary ways is the much younger Rails-to-Trails Conservancy. This is the outfit greatly responsible for transforming thousands of miles of former rail corridor across the nation to paths for human-powered travel. The more than seven hundred individual trails vary in length from just a few miles to hundreds. Most of the surfaces are a fine chip gravel over a very hard base, which makes them palatable for thin tires and perfect for fat. Your very small annual membership dues, multiplied by millions of riders, help to support the continued fight to secure and develop these pathways. (Address and phone in the appendix.)

There is a last source of information about mountain bike trails across the United States and Canada that I want to mention, of which I am the senior editor. This is the only national series of mountain bike guides currently in existence, a coast-to-coast compendium of each state and region's "classic" fat-tire trails, researched and written by fellow riders who also provide the other kinds of information of value to us: availability of water, services in nearby towns, bike shops that cater to mountain bikers, and various sources of additional information about the trail or other riding in the area. These *Dennis Coello's America by Mountain Bike Series* books are copublished by Menasha Ridge Press and Falcon Press, and can be ordered by calling the publishers at the numbers in the appendix.

▪ MOUNTAIN BIKE TOUR COMPANIES ▪

Does it all sound a bit too much? The gathering of equipment, the choice of trails, learning to do the repairs in case of breakdown?

Tour companies are one way to ease into backcountry bike travel. You can call for a catalog, choose a trip, send them a check, and worry after that about nothing but getting in shape. You don't even have to get your bike in shape, or even *have* one for that matter; if you choose to rent one, most companies have them available.

There are other reasons that tens of thousands of mountain bikers each year travel dirt roads and trails with tour companies. One is time, or rather not enough of it to plan the tour yourself. Another is a preference, after solving problems and dealing with hassles all day at work and home, to let someone else be ultimately responsible for problems on the ride. Which leaves you only the tasks of pedaling and enjoying yourself.

There are scores of touring companies, as you'll learn when you look in the back of bike magazines. The list in the appendix is of those I've pedaled with in North America and abroad. Like the people they cater to, all companies aren't the same. But I'd ride again with all of them. Call for free catalogs. They will give you something to dream about during your coffee breaks at work.

Cyclist on an organized tour through south China.

▪ EQUIPMENT CHECKLIST ▪

The following is a basic checklist of the gear I pack when touring. It is added to considerably when tours are long, or when they take place during cold weather; it is subtracted from when riding single overnights. I alter it also for desert tours, for mountain treks, for swamp rides in Louisiana, for tours when I expect to be in towns a lot. My point is that this should serve as a guide, not a recipe guaranteed to fill your every need or keep you from packing what you won't require.

Quantity—the number of T-shirts or cycling shorts for a summer ride, for instance—will be determined, of course, by the tour length, by the load you want to carry, and by how willing you are to wash out clothes each evening.

Shelter and Bedding

tent or bivy sack
sleeping bag
ground pad

Clothing

T-shirts (replaced by wicking, long-sleeve underwear if cold)
long-sleeve shirt or sweatshirt
cycling shorts
noncycling shorts (like Patagonia Baggies)
undershorts
long pants (fall/winter tours only, if in towns a lot)
insulated underwear
leg warmers/tights
socks
cycling shoes/boots
camp moccasins
riding gloves

Be prepared for all kinds of weather.

Foul- and Cold-Weather Gear

shoe covers/overboots

Gore-Tex socks

gaiters

neck gaiter

ear gaiter

helmet liner

stocking cap

face mask

gloves

waterproof overmitts/overgloves

poncho/chaps or rainsuit

goggles

vest

toe covers (over toe clips)

Personal Items

towel (I prefer the Pak Towels by Cascade Designs, for their absorption
    and durability)

washcloth

soap (biodegradable)/soap dish

toothbrush/case

floss

comb

toilet paper (partial roll)

deodorant

shampoo (biodegradable)

waterless hand cleaner

nailbrush

fingernail clipper

Tools and Spare Parts

See chapter 2, page 65 for this list. A discussion of each tool appears in
chapter 7.

Medical Supplies

See the list provided earlier in this chapter, and also in chapter 2. Do
not forget to add water purification tablets.

Miscellaneous

helmet

sunglasses

pocketknife

map/compass

headlamp/batteries and/or candle lantern/candles

parachute cord

ripstop repair tape

waterproof matches (or kitchen matches in waterproof container)

book

notebook

pen

pants clips

trowel

thread (heavy duty)/needle

panniers/pannier covers

handlebar bag/seat bag

water bottles

insect repellent

whistle

signal mirror

Cooking Supplies

stove/fuel bottle

pot/lid

pot gripper

plastic cup

utensils (Lexan plastic)

sponge/scrub pad

Mountain bike, boot, and bird tracks across snow.

6

THE ATB CONTROVERSY: TRAIL ETIQUETTE AND WILDERNESS PROTECTION

This is surely the most explosive issue in mountain biking, so let's begin with the history of the conflict. In 1964, in an attempt to "establish a National Wilderness Preservation system for the permanent good of the whole people," the U.S. Congress passed the Wilderness Act. Designated lands were to be set aside, to remain *natural*—pure, pristine, and uncontaminated.

To guard against the erosion of this natural condition, Section 4(c) of the act stated:

> . . . there shall be no temporary road, no use of motor vehicles, motorized equipment or motor boats, no landing aircraft, no other form of mechanical transport, and no structure . . . within such area.

Today, Section 4(c) of the Wilderness Act remains unchanged.

Yet in 1964, mountain bikes had not yet been born.

Although mountain bikes are not motorized, they are a "form of mechanical transport," and as such are excluded. For a time there was confusion on this issue, primarily as a result of the Forest Service regulations set forth in 1965 for those lands under Department of Agriculture jurisdiction. In the Code of Federal Regulations (CFR) Section 293.6(a), "mechanical transport" is defined as:

> . . . any contrivance which travels over ground . . . on wheels . . . and is
> propelled by a non-living power source . . . contained or carried . . . on the
> device.

Mountain bikers read this, checked to see if they were still *living* power sources, and concluded their vehicles were therefore allowed in Department of Agriculture–administered wilderness areas. But in 1983 Forest Service Chief Max Peterson did away with this confusion by stating the Wilderness Act regulatory language was applicable to *all* wildernesses—and thereby prohibited the use of mountain bikes in any wilderness area whatsoever. The fact that we are indeed living power sources is of no consequence.

Some cyclists still hope for a revision of the Wilderness Act prohibition, arguing that if ATBs had been around in 1964 their use would have been allowed. Ed Bloedel, of the U.S. Forest Service in Washington, D.C., is perhaps representative of the opposite position and gives his reasons:

> It's the cumulative effect of things like this that really hurt our national
> wilderness system. Once you begin making little exceptions here and
> there you begin to lose what you're trying to provide in the first place—
> a chunk of primitive America, of something that is essentially the same as
> our forefathers found it.

It took eight years of wrangling for Congress to pass the Wilderness Act, and any change to allow the use of mountain bikes would bring about a firestorm of protest and intense lobbying efforts by individuals and environmental organizations. Sally Reid, a Sierra Club officer, says, "If you think bicycles can get into the Wilderness Act, you just don't know how the United States feels about it, about that act. Nobody is going to monkey with that. There would be an uproar if anyone tried to open up wilderness areas to vehicles."

Today, therefore, and for the foreseeable future, mountain bikes are not permitted in:

a) wilderness areas

b) national parks (except on roads, and those paths specifically marked BIKE PATH)

c) national monuments (except on roads open to the public)

d) most state parks and monuments (except on roads, and those paths specifically marked BIKE PATH)

e) an increasing number of urban and county parks, especially in California (except on roads, and those paths specifically marked BIKE PATH)

The use of ATBs is at present allowed on national forest roads and trails, except for those in wilderness or primitive areas, and on those trails marked with signs declaring NO BIKES ALLOWED, or declared off-limits to bikes on the appropriate "travel map." (Travel maps showing permissible vehicular use are available from national forest local district offices.) Of the approximately 100,000 miles of trails in national forests, roughly 32,000 are in wilderness areas.

The use of ATBs is at present allowed on Bureau of Land Management (BLM) lands. BLM administers 334 million acres nationally. Some of the regions have seasonal limited-use restrictions, due to possible animal disturbance. And some have signs requiring road travel only, due to fragile ecosystems.

The Sierra Club, as one of many environmental organizations opposed to mountain bike use in wilderness areas and on some other lands, amended its previous (and similar) position by adopting the following Policy on Off-Road Use of Vehicles in May '88:

> The Sierra Club reaffirms its support for the Wilderness Act's prohibition of "mechanized modes of transport," including non-motorized vehicles, from entry into designated wilderness.

Concerning "use of vehicles on other public lands":

> Trails and areas on public lands should be closed to all vehicles unless: (1) determined to be appropriate for their use through completion of an analysis, review, and implementation process; and (2) officially posted with signs as being open.

> The process must include: (1) application of objective criteria to assess whether or not environmental quality can be effectively maintained, and whether the safety and enjoyment of all users can be protected; (2) a public review and comment procedure involving all interested parties; and (3) promulgation of effective implementing regulations where impacts are sufficiently low that vehicle use is appropriate.

> Trails and areas designated for vehicular use must be monitored periodically to detect environmental damage or user interference inconsistent with the above criteria. Where this occurs, the trail or area must be closed to vehicles unless effective corrective regulations are enforced.

The topics of "environmental damage" and "user interference" are continuing sources of disagreement. Many mountain bikers contend that the few trail-impact studies that have been done indicate their impact is far less damaging than that of horses, and that it is the very few "kamikaze" riders who tear up the soil, frighten animals, and bother fellow trail-users who give all mountain bikers a bad name.

In an attempt to defuse the conflict between cyclists and hiker/equestrians (and thereby deter further trail closings to mountain bikes), many national off-road bicycle organizations have formed, and are providing guidelines to their members for safe, responsible trail use. One of the largest of these—National Off-Road Bicycle Association (NORBA)—publishes the following suggested code of behavior for mountain bikers:

1. I will yield the right of way to other non-motorized recreationists. I realize that people judge all cyclists by my actions.

2. I will slow down and use caution when approaching or overtaking another and will make my presence known well in advance.

3. I will maintain control of my speed at all times and will approach turns in anticipation of someone around the bend.

4. I will stay on designated trails to avoid trampling native vegetation and minimize potential erosion to trails by not using muddy trails or short-cutting switchbacks.

5. I will not disturb wildlife or livestock.

6. I will not litter. I will pack out what I pack in, and pack out more than my share whenever possible.

7. I will respect public and private property, including trail use signs, no trespassing signs, and I will leave gates as I have found them.

8. I will always be self-sufficient and my destination and travel speed will be determined by my ability, my equipment, the terrain, the present and potential weather conditions.

9. I will not travel solo when bikepacking in remote areas. I will leave word of my destination and when I plan to return.

10. I will observe the practice of minimum impact bicycling by "taking only pictures and memories and leaving only waffle prints."

11. I will always wear a helmet whenever I ride.

I have a problem with number nine. The most enjoyable mountain biking I've ever done has been solo. And as for leaving word of my destination and time of return, I've enjoyed living in such a way as to say, "I'm off to pedal Colorado. See you in the fall." Of course it's senseless to take needless risks, and I plan a ride and pack my gear with this in mind. And getting away from civilization, deep into the wilds, is, for many people, what mountain biking's all about.

All in all, however, theirs is a good list, and surely we mountain bikers would be liked more, and excluded less, if we followed their suggestions. But let me offer a "code of ethics" I much prefer, one given to cyclists by Utah's Wasatch-Cache National Forest Office:

> *Study a Forest Map Before You Ride:* Currently, bicycles are permitted on roads and developed trails within the Wasatch-Cache National Forest except in designated Wilderness. If your route crosses private land, it is your responsibility to obtain right-of-way permission from the owner.

All mountain bikers are judged by the actions of one, so respect private property.

Keep Groups Small: Riding in large groups degrades the outdoor experience for others, can disturb wildlife, and usually leads to greater resource damage.

Avoid Riding on Wet Trails: Bicycle tires leave ruts in wet trails. These ruts concentrate runoff and accelerate erosion. Postponing a ride when the trails are wet will preserve the trails for future use.

Stay on Roads and Trails: Riding cross-country destroys vegetation and damages the soil.

Always Yield to Others: Trails are shared by hikers, horses, and bicycles. Move off the trail to allow horses to pass and stop to allow hikers adequate room to share the trail. Simply yelling "Bicycle" is not acceptable.

Control Your Speed: Excessive speed endangers yourself and other forest users.

Avoid Wheel Lockup and Spinout: Steep terrain is especially vulnerable to trail wear. Locking brakes on steep descents, or when stopping, needlessly damages trails. If a slope is steep enough to require locking wheels and skidding, dismount and walk your bicycle. Likewise, if an ascent is so steep your rear wheel slips and spins, dismount and walk your bicycle.

Protect Water Bars and Switchbacks: Water bars—the rock and log drains built to direct water off trails—protect trails from erosion. When you encounter a water bar, ride directly over the top or dismount and walk your bicycle. Riding around the ends of water bars destroys them and speeds erosion. Skidding around switchback

Biker spooking cattle on Lost Valley Trail.

corners shortens trail life. Slow for switchback corners and keep your wheels rolling.

If You Abuse It, You Lose It: Mountain bikes are relative new-comers to the forest and must prove themselves responsible trail users. By following the guidelines above, and by participating in trail maintenance service projects, bicyclists can help avoid closures that would prevent them from using trails.

Well, so much for the relevant facts. The arguments and issues surrounding the ATB-in-the-wilderness controversy are many and varied, sometimes (as the saying goes) generating more heat than light. One thing is certain: Most mountain bikers want to enjoy and maintain the pristine environment championed by conservationists. The exceptions are the "banzai" or "kamikaze" riders who race along the trails spooking animals and humans, and who deserve what they get when slamming into trees or when ticketed by rangers or knocked off their bikes by fellow bikers and hikers.

Of course, opinions vary widely. NORBA Director Chris Ross stresses the fact that most of his members are following NORBA's eleven-point code and that a few bad apples are distorting the bikers' image: "For every two hundred people who follow the code, it only takes one or two banzai guys to ruin things. No one notices all the rest who do no damage; they only notice those who do it wrong."

Sierra Club officer Sally Reid takes a similar tack for non-wilderness trails: "Trails must be analyzed by land managers for their appropriateness for bicycle use. . . .Obviously there are trails which should be left open [to mountain bikers]; I have no objection to bicycles on trails where I can see them, and where they can see me."

But on the issue of opening federally designated wilderness areas to mountain bikers, Reid is unequivocal: "No. It's too disturbing to animals. It's too disturbing to people. It's too disturbing to vegetation. Just no!"

There are, it seems, almost as many positions on the issue as there are people willing to voice an opinion. I accept the validity of many parts of the arguments put forth by those who wish a change in the Wilderness Act. I also see the inherent difficulties in the Sierra Club proposal that public land trails be excluded until opened to bikes, rather than the reverse (which is true at present).

I know these things from my many conversations with fellow cyclists around the nation, and with the many Forest Service and Park Service per-

. . . but at what price to the environment?

sonnel I meet during my annual two-wheeled travels. I would also love to see more of these wilderness regions than those few miles I can reach on a day hike, and would prefer my bike-and-hike approach to that of long treks in and out with great weight on my back. All these desires would seem to put me squarely in the camp of those of my fellow mountain bikers who would welcome wilderness areas open to us.

Nevertheless, I continue to *support* our wilderness exclusion. My reasons are not primarily environmental, given my view that most mountain bikers are concerned about damage, and that "tender" soils—at least in the steeper and harder-to-reach wilderness regions—attract few bikers anyway. No, it is almost exclusively for aesthetic reasons that I hope to see our banishment continued. Despite the arguments of how mechanical modern packs or skis or high-tech stoves may be, or how unappealing it is to follow a trail recently traveled by a pack train and horses—and humans with

Mountain biker using Jeep road.

backpacks—they do not detract from the natural experience that I believe wilderness areas must protect. And mountain bikes, I sincerely believe, do. For me there's no getting around the fact that a bike is a vehicle. And it's as out of place in the wilderness as a horse would be as a mount for your urban commute.

I support the Sierra Club policy of "trail studies first, *then* official openings." There is a risk of doing too much damage to some environmentally sensitive trails. My Forest Service friends contend they have enough to do as it is, but I believe it would not be impossible—in, say, a year to eighteen months—to determine the status of at least our most-used trails.

We might be forced off our favorite single-tracks for a season during the assessment process, and made to satisfy ourselves with jeep roads and other routes. For that matter, we may lose access to a few of our favorite trails forever, especially if they are close to towns and thus put us in conflict with fellow users. But I honestly believe this process would mean the preservation and *permanent* opening of far more trail miles to us in future.

(See the appendix for the International Mountain Bicycling Association's (IMBA'S) Rules of the Trail.)

MAINTENANCE AND REPAIR

Mountain bike manufacturers, knowing how their rigs are beaten about and generally mistreated, have produced amazingly durable bikes that require little effort to keep in good working order. Almost everything is obvious on a mountain bike; most components can be removed with a simple Allen (hex) wrench; wheels are wider and shorter than those found on spindly thin-tire bikes, requiring far less care regardless of the trail bashing they take; little on a beefy ATB is so delicate that it will break if handled somewhat incorrectly when you first attempt repair. And as for those things that are more difficult to reach—the sealed bearings hiding away in pedals, wheel hubs, headsets, and bottom brackets—I'll show you how to reach them for the infrequent times when they require service. But, because they are sealed, you can go a very long time between cleanings.

In short, you don't have to be a mechanic to maintain a mountain bike, or to follow the simple instructions in this chapter. If you, like me, have not been blessed with mechanical aptitude, or if you do possess such a mind but simply haven't yet been schooled in which end of a wrench does the work, much of the following at first glance will appear impossible to master. But, then, so did learning to tie your shoes.

So take it easy, and *slowly*. Read the procedures with the bike in front of you; otherwise you'll be lost. Remember that it's all mechanical, that you can *see* what's happening when you turn a screw or tighten a spoke. Don't give up at the first hint of confusion. And if at some point you do have to wheel your rig to the bike shop for expert care, ask the man or woman in the mechanic's apron if you can watch.

▪ TOOLS ▪

As mentioned in earlier chapters, most commuters and trail riders out for a day pack only a set of Allen wrenches, six-inch crescent, small screwdriver, tire levers, air pump, and a spare tube and patch kit. And more and more are replacing many of these with a single minitool. The following list, however, and the accompanying drawing, includes both my on-the-road and my at-home tools.

1. *Fifteen-inch crescent wrench:* I far prefer a vise to pull my freewheel, but this does a good job of it and is far less expensive. When at home I use it in place of my pocket vise or cassette cracker, and also instead of my six-inch crescent for pulling off a cotterless crank (the six-inch must be used on the road, but the strain on this small tool is great). Home only.

2. *Six-inch crescent wrench:* Once the most used tool by cyclists, but now replaced in that category by Allen wrenches when it comes to mountain bikes. Be sure to buy one of good quality; the slide mechanism on a cheap one will in time refuse to stay cinched tightly against a nut.

3. *Four-inch crescent wrench:* Very nice for brake work, if you

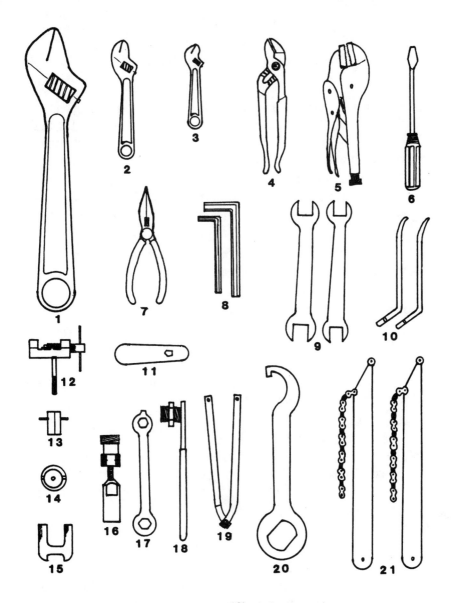

1) crescent wrench—15″
2) crescent wrench—6″
3) crescent wrench—4″
4) channel locks—7″
5) vise grips
6) regular blade screwdriver
7) needle-nose pliers
8) Allen wrenches
9) cone wrenches
10) tire levers
11) Swiss Army Knife
12) chain rivet tool
13) spoke nipple wrench
14) freewheel tool
15) pocket vise
16) cotterless crank removal tool
17) universal cotterless crankarm wrench
18) universal cotterless crankarm puller
19) universal adjustable cup tool
20) lock ring/fixed cup bottom bracket tool
21) freewheel sprocket tools

don't plan to purchase a set of metric open or box ends. Remember that this tool, like so many others pictured, will not be carried on the road and isn't really necessary for home repair. It's included simply because it makes some jobs easier than do the larger wrenches.

4. *Seven-inch channel lock:* This is an excellent road tool for tightening headsets, and for gripping anything too large for the six-inch crescent. It is part of my personal commuting/day-riding/touring kit.

5. *Vise grips:* A larger pair is required to remove blips from rim walls, something you may never need to do if you're lucky and keep your tires properly inflated. Home only.

6. *Regular-blade screwdriver:* I pack a thin, lightweight, short-handled screwdriver that, with long shank included, measures six inches in length; the flat blade tip (only $3/16$-inch wide) is perfect for very fine adjustments of derailleur set screws. Buy a poor quality screwdriver and the blade will bend and chip in no time.

7. *Needle-nose pliers:* I prefer a small pair with side-cutters (for trimming brake and gear cables). Home only.

8. *Allen (hex) wrenches:* Do not leave on a long ride without making sure you have an Allen for each and every size Allen head on the bike, for the Fates will surely cause that single bolt you've overlooked to loosen up. Also, do not try to get by with an Allen wrench that "almost" fits; you'll end up rounding off the inside corners and ruining the bolt.

9. *Cone wrenches:* Make sure they are thin and lightweight, and that they fit your cones. The far heavier shop models are for home use only.

10. *Tire levers:* I pack only two; I find the third one sold in most sets to be unnecessary. The tips must be perfectly smooth, or you'll be puncturing your tube while trying to repair it.

11. *Swiss Army knife:* Extremely handy for many reasons on multi-week backcountry tours; large models not worth the weight on shorter rides.

12. *Chain rivet tool:* Necessary for removing a chain, adding links, and freeing frozen links. Be sure the rivet tool you're buying will fit the chain on your bike.

13. *Spoke nipple wrench:* The "T"-type is pictured; this model and the "hoop"-style wrench are my preferences over the round multisize nipple wrenches. Make sure the wrench you purchase will fit your spokes.

14. *Freewheel tool:* Those riders still equipped with old-style freewheels will need to pack along the specific freewheel tool that fits their freewheel, but only on extended backcountry tours. Much more common today are freehubs or cassette freewheels, where a specific freewheel tool is still required (to remove the lock ring sitting outside the smallest sprocket), plus a freewheel sprocket tool (too large to carry easily) or a very portable "cassette cracker" device to remove the sprockets and allow access to freewheel-side spokes for replacement. A 10 mm hex wrench is required to remove the freewheel "body" or "core" from the wheel.

15. *Pocket vise:* This wonderful creation is necessary—along with the freewheel tool above—for most freewheel removals on the road. It serves the same purpose as a cassette cracker for freehubs. Let me say again that very, very few of you will ever break a spoke, making this tool unnecessary.

16. *Cotterless crank removal tool:* Again, make sure it fits your bike. I carry this with me always, but few people make it part of their commuting or short trail riding kit.

17. *Universal cotterless crank wrench:* For use with the following item (number 18); home tool only, and only if you work on several cranks of different sizes.

18. *Universal cotterless crankarm puller:* The cotterless crank wrench removes the crankarm fixing bolt (that wonderful advance in technology beyond the formerly ubiquitous cotter pins); this tool pulls the crankarm to allow access to the bottom bracket hub. Home only.

19. *Universal adjustable cup tool:* This is excellent for home use, but far too heavy for the road. Only on my longest tours do I work on my bottom bracket, and then I use a screwdriver blade tip to adjust the bottom bracket bearing pressure.

20. *Lock ring/fixed cup bottom bracket tool:* For adjustments of the bottom bracket lock ring and fixed cup; home use only.

21. *Freewheel sprocket tools:* Home use. If you have a large vise, you'll need only one; two are otherwise required to change sprockets. Most people toss their entire freewheels when only a couple of cogs need replacing (the smallest two, usually, if you do a lot of commuting or dirt-road riding)—a far less expensive repair than buying all new sprockets plus the center core body filled with ball bearings.

22. *Sealed bearing tools:* As you've already learned, most mountain bikes have sealed bearings somewhere—in pedals, headset, hubs, bottom bracket. Many of these seals can be removed easily with one or more of the tools above, or very carefully with a thin knife blade, but some are more conveniently removed with specific tools for this purpose. Your dealer will point out these seals to you, and will either have the appropriate tool for sale or can order it. Don't be afraid to ask to be shown how to use it, but be prepared to return to the shop at some time convenient to *them.* Don't expect free instructions during busy Friday afternoons and Saturdays.

Beyond the tools listed above, tune-up stands of many kinds are available, plus wheel-trueing stands that make the job far easier. Finally, a floor pump with built-in gauge and flip-off air nozzle is a must if you ride daily.

▪ SADDLE ▪

A good bike shop will help you determine general saddle position when sizing you for your bike, but most riders find slight adjustments of height, tilt, and position toward or away from the handlebars necessary to produce that perfect fit of cycle and cyclist. The quick-release (q-r) lever will allow extremely fast changes in saddle height, and most mountain bike seatposts require only an Allen wrench to alter tilt and forward/aft position.

Height

First, flip the q-r lever. Second, adjust the saddle height. Third, close the q-r lever tightly. Done.

Tilt

Saddle tilt is an individual preference. I suggest you begin with no
slant whatsoever, and work from
there. You need merely loosen the
beneath-the-saddle Allen fittings,
position the saddle as desired, and
tighten.

Forward/Backward Movement

You'll recall I mentioned this in the
earlier discussion of bike fit (see
page 22). The saddle has the ability
to move toward or away from the
handlebars along its "rails" (look
beneath the saddle for these). This
distance, plus top tube and handlebar stem length, allows an extremely personal fit. Pay attention to
slight arm, neck, and lower back

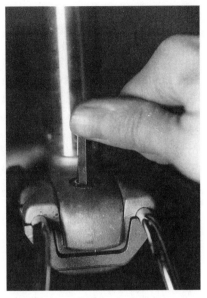

Under the saddle Allen head adjustment
bolt (for changing tilt and for/aft position of saddle).

strain if you are too far from or too close to the bars, and adjust accordingly. Remember that a good bike shop will provide a general fit, but you must
tailor it precisely to your own body and riding style. Again, simply loosen
the Allen bolt or bolts beneath the saddle, slide the saddle along its rails,
and tighten again.

Side-to-Side Movement

The saddle nose should, of course, point directly over the top tube. If it has
worked itself off-center, flip the quick-release seatpost bolt, position correctly,
then close tightly.

▪ HANDLEBAR/HEADSET ▪

Don't be scared by all the parts of a headset; chances are excellent, especially with the ATB's sealed (or "shielded") bearings, that you'll never have

to deal with them out on the road or trail. Most riders never work on their headsets, except when erroneously thinking it necessary to raise or lower the handlebars. The following words are provided, therefore, to help you understand this usually neglected portion of your bike, and to facilitate adjustments and repairs if necessary.

First, the headset's job is not to hold the handlebar in place. (This is done by the bar's own expander bolt/wedge assembly, as you'll soon see.) Its purpose is to secure the fork to the frame in such a manner as to allow free rotation to the right and left. Now look closely at the drawing and you'll see how this is performed. The top of the fork is threaded, and is held in place in the head tube by the top threaded race (bearing cup). This race, and the fork crown race, is positioned with the top and bottom bearings to allow for rotation. In all my riding the greatest difficulty I've had with headsets (a slight difficulty in turning the bars side to side) was remedied in the following fifteen-minute repair.

A   B   C   D   E   F   G   D   H   I

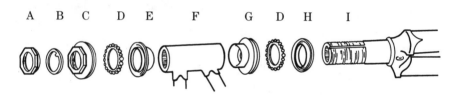

A) locknut
B) lock washer
C) adjusting cup/top threaded race
D) bearings
E) top head/set race

F) head tube
G) bottom head/set race
H) fork crown race
I) fork

First, using my large crescent when at home, or the channel locks on the road, I loosen the large locknut at the top of the headset. Next, I loosen the top threaded race, but only slightly, until I can see the bearings inside but *before* they can escape (something that won't happen if you have the ball retainer rings common to many bikes today, and especially if they are sealed). I then squirt cycle oil into the mass of bearings, very carefully allow the fork to slip down a fraction of an inch to expose the bottom bearings, and add oil there. This done, I tighten the top threaded race, then the locknut on top, until there is no upward or downward movement within the headset, but free movement of the fork side to side.

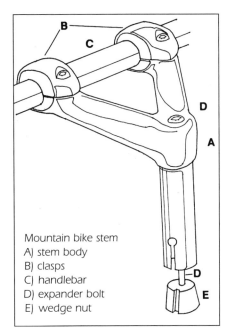

Mountain bike stem
A) stem body
B) clasps
C) handlebar
D) expander bolt
E) wedge nut

External wedge.

Bar Height Adjustment

Notice the expander bolt in the drawing. At the other end of this bolt—inside the head tube—is either an angled expander nut or a wedge nut (an "exterior" or "interior" wedge). When the expander bolt is tightened, the angled nut presses against the head tube wall; the wedge nut–type works by drawing the nut up inside the stem, forcing the stem walls out against the head tube.

Now take the second important step in all mechanical repairs: a *close* look at everything that might be affected or at all involved. In the case of lowering or raising bars, many brake assemblies are involved (through the lengthening or shortening of the brake cable). If this is so with your bars, simply disengage the brake cable until the bar is adjusted, then readjust cable length.

Loosen the expander bolt. Don't be concerned if the wedge nut comes off the expander bolt; it can't fall far. Just turn the bike upside down and the nut will come free. If your bike is brand new, your bars can be moved when the expander bolt is loosened. If not, you'll have to rethread the expander bolt a couple of turns into the frozen angled or wedge nut inside the head tube, and then rap it lightly with a mallet (or something similar). Position the bars as desired—being absolutely sure to leave at least two full inches of stem inside the head tube (even more critical on a mountain bike, due to the tremendous beating the handlebars take)—and tighten the expander bolt.

Bars Off Center

Sometimes a fall will cause the bars not to point straight over the wheel. In this case simply loosen the expander bolt assembly (as above), reposition, and tighten securely.

Loose Brake Lever

On a mountain bike the Allen head fitting is easy to see; reposition and tighten.

▪ BRAKES ▪

A thorough study of these assemblies will go far in reducing any fears in working on them. You will see a cable leading from the brake handle, through a cable adjustment of some kind, to the wheel brake component. When the hand brake is squeezed, the cable length is shortened, pulling the brake pads toward the wheel rim until contact is made.

Difficulties are encountered when, after much use, the brake pads have worn down, or the cable has stretched, becoming slightly rusted inside its housing, or broken. The first two problems are remedied with no tools at all, and can, in fact, be accomplished from the saddle.

Worn Pads and Cable Stretch

Look back to your cable adjustment assembly, where an adjustment barrel of one shape or another shortens the cable when turned counterclockwise; a locknut or lock ring beneath the barrel must be loosened to allow adjustment, then tightened again to hold the barrel in place.

After many miles a cable might require more adjustment than what's possible through these assemblies. In this case, begin by screwing down the barrel completely (to allow for greater adjustments later), then loosen the cable anchor bolt (it will be obvious which bolt and nut combination holds

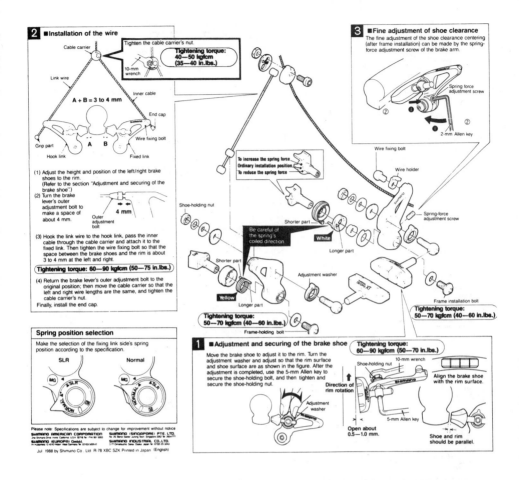

2 ■Installation of the wire

Cable carrier

Tighten the cable carrier's nut.

**Tightening torque:
40—50 kgfcm
(35—40 in.lbs.)**

10-mm wrench

Link wire

Inner cable

A + B = 3 to 4 mm

End cap

Grip part

Hook link

A B

Fixed link

Wire fixing bolt

(1) Adjust the height and position of the left/right brake shoes to the rim.
(Refer to the section "Adjustment and securing of the brake shoe".)
(2) Turn the brake lever's outer adjustment bolt to make a space of about 4 mm.

4 mm

Outer adjustment bolt

(3) Hook the link wire to the hook link, pass the inner cable through the cable carrier and attach it to the fixed link. Then tighten the wire fixing bolt so that the space between the brake shoes and the rim is about 3 to 4 mm at the left and right.

Tightening torque: 60—90 kgfcm (50—75 in.lbs.)

(4) Return the brake lever's outer adjustment bolt to the original position; then move the cable carrier so that the left and right wire lengths are the same, and tighten the cable carrier's nut.
Finally, install the end cap.

Spring position selection

Make the selection of the fixing link side's spring position according to the specification.

SLR

Normal

Please note Specifications are subject to change for improvement without notice

SHIMANO AMERICAN CORPORATION   SHIMANO (SINGAPORE) PTE. LTD.
SHIMANO (EUROPA) GmbH   SHIMANO INDUSTRIAL CO. LTD.

Jul 1988 by Shimano Co., Ltd. R-78 XBC SZK Printed in Japan (English)

3 ■Fine adjustment of shoe clearance

The fine adjustment of the shoe clearance centering (after frame installation) can be made by the spring-force adjustment screw of the brake arm.

Spring force adjustment screw

2-mm Allen key

Wire fixing bolt

Wire holder

To increase the spring force
Ordinary installation position
To reduce the spring force

Spring-force adjustment screw

Shoe-holding nut

Shorter part

Be careful of the spring's coiled direction.

White

Longer part

Shorter part

Adjustment washer

Frame installation bolt

**Tightening torque:
50—70 kgfcm (40—60 in.lbs.)**

Yellow

Longer part

**Tightening torque:
50—70 kgfcm (40—60 in.lbs.)**

Frame-holding bolt

1 ■Adjustment and securing of the brake shoe

**Tightening torque:
60—90 kgfcm (50—70 in.lbs.)**

Move the brake shoe to adjust it to the rim. Turn the adjustment washer and adjust so that the rim surface and shoe surface are as shown in the figure. After the adjustment is completed, use the 5-mm Allen key to secure the shoe-holding bolt, and then tighten and secure the shoe-holding nut.

Shoe-holding nut

10-mm wrench

Align the brake shoe with the rim surface.

Direction of rim rotation

Adjustment washer

5-mm Allen key

Open about 0.5—1.0 mm.

Shoe and rim should be parallel.

These detailed drawings and instructions (courtesy of Shimano) will help you adjust and/or repair your bike no matter its brand of componetry. Again, go slowly and logically from step to step.

the cable in place, as the cable passes directly through it). Ideally, this should be done with the brake pads pressed against the rim, so as to estimate proper cable position. A third-hand tool may be used for this purpose, or a fellow rider. But far more often I simply squeeze the pads together, toward the rim, then lift free one end of the short transverse cable (also called center wire or link wire)—

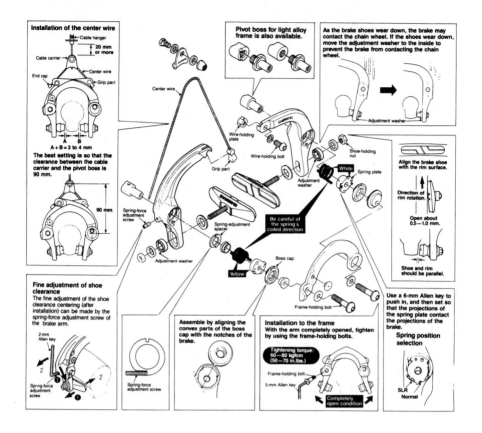

Courtesy Shimano (installation of U-brake)

the cable running between the tops of either brake arm, at the end of the long brake cable stretching from the brake handle to the brake assembly on the wheel. Normally this technique is used to allow for the fast removal of tires, as this moves the brake pads away from the rim sufficiently to enable the larger tire profile to pass. But when adjusting brakes I do it so as to loosen the cable anchor bolt, take up a slight amount of slack cable, tighten the cable anchor bolt again, and reset the brake. It's seldom perfectly correct the first time around, but usually very close on the second.

Brake pads, by the way, should be set close enough to the rim to ensure the fast, strong application of brake pad force against the rim with only the slightest movement of the brake handle. With poorly adjusted brakes, a precious second is lost while cable slack is taken up through the hard squeezing of the brake handle. Not only can this delay in reaction time be costly, but also the pressure of pad against rim will be reduced. Naturally, a well-aligned wheel is necessary if pads are to be mounted close to the rim.

Rubber brake pads once came mounted in their metal "shoes" in such a way that replacement pads were easily installed. The shoes had one end open—the end, of course, that was intended to be mounted *against* the direction of wheel rotation (open end toward the back of the bike, in other words). Otherwise the pads would merely shoot forward out of their shoes, leaving you to white-knuckle your way to a thrilling, unassisted stop. Most shoe/pad arrangements today are a single piece, which unfortunately requires a more costly replacement. Just be thoughtful during the replacement if you have the older style.

Adjustment of the Shimano U-brake is explained by that company's artwork; the SunTour roller cam cable or brake arm tension (for those few riders still using them) is adjusted easily with the roller cam brake tool (now difficult to find, due to SunTour's demise) holding the brake arms (and thus the pads) in place.

Cable Replacement/Lubrication

Watch carefully as you remove the broken cable from its housing and you'll learn almost all you need to know for replacement. Notice the ball (or pear- or cylinder-shaped) end of the cable, held in place by the brake handle housing. Brake cables come with one end that will fit your particular housing; the other end is to be cut off (carefully, so that individual metal strands don't fray) to allow its placement into the cable housing, and final entry into the tiny hole in the cable anchor bolt, or far more easily laid into the slotted washer groove. (I use the side-cutter portion of my needle-nose pliers for this cut when at home, but as I do not carry a needle-nose any longer on the road, on occasion I have had to resort to more barbaric means. I first crimp the cable strands by placing my screwdriver blade over the cable and tapping the other end with a wrench. Then I work the metal strands back and forth with the channel locks, until the strands break. Or, far more simply, buy just the cable that will fit your particular brake, or have the foresight to clip off the proper end before you pack your tool kit. If you buy a new bike, however, be sure your old cable will fit.)

Once having depressed the brake handle and located the barrel end of the broken cable, remove the brake cable. Snip off the unnecessary end of the new cable, lightly grease the cable throughout its length, then insert it beneath the brake handle and into the cable housing. Run its cut end through the cable anchor bolt, and adjust pad placement as discussed above. Excess cable can be wound into a ball or cut off.

Sometimes a slight crack in the cable housing, or a drop of water that manages to find its way inside, will cause brakes to stick. Although the metal brake arms are usually suspected (a drop or two of oil will keep these working well, and can be applied now to determine if these arms or the cable is at fault), it is more likely that rust has formed inside the housing. Simply release the cable at the cable anchor bolt, slip it completely out of its housing, grease, and reattach. (This will be much easier if the free, cut end of the cable has been kept from fraying by a tiny metal cable clamp—a soft metal cup that is slipped over the cable end and secured by a squeeze with the channel locks or needle-nose pliers.)

You must be sure, of course, that when the brakes are depressed the pads strike the rim entirely. This is especially critical with U-brakes, because when misadjusted the pads move up and into the tire (thereby cutting into the tire wall), rather than down and away from the tire and rim, as with cantilever brakes.

A final adjustment required with many brakes is the toe-in of brake pads. Look closely at your pads when new and you can see if yours are set in this manner. If they are, you will notice that the portion of the pad closer to the front of the bike strikes the rim first (as shown in the U-brake adjustment drawing).

▪ TIRES/SPOKES/WHEEL ALIGNMENT ▪

The wheel consists of many parts: hub assembly, spokes, freewheel (or freehub and cogs), rim, rim tape (a cloth, plastic, or rubber strip covering the spoke heads, thus protecting the tube from the spokes), tube, tire, and sometimes tire liner (which I suggest for commuting and cactus-area riding). On-the-road repairs required by these parts are usually caused by flat tires and wheels out of alignment. Spoke breakage is extremely infrequent, but will be covered just to put the mind at ease.

Flats

When the cursing is over, assemble the necessary tools: two tire levers, a six-inch crescent (if your wheels aren't quick-release), tube repair kit or spare tube, and air pump.

A.

B.

C.

1. Remove the wheel. (Photo A) To do so, put your bike on its back, loosen both axle nuts or trip the quick-release lever, and disengage the short transverse (or center or link wire) brake cable—to increase the distance between the brake pads sufficiently for the tire to pass between them. (This is the cable running between the top of either brake arm, and to which the main brake cable is attached. (Photo B.) Squeeze the pads toward the rim to lift one end of the transverse cable free, as explained in the previous repair procedure.) If it's the front wheel, simply lift the wheel out of its dropouts at this point. On the rear wheel, shift the chain into the smallest freewheel sprocket, grab the derailleur body and pull it toward the rear of the bike, and lift the wheel free. (Photo C.)

D.

E.

F.

2. Remove the tire and tube from the rim. This is accomplished with the aid of your tire levers (or spoons). Take the lesser angled end of one spoon and, beveled end up, work it underneath the tire bead about half an inch. (Photo D.) (Begin working with the first lever at a point on the wheel opposite to the valve stem.) Now push down (toward the spokes) on the tire lever in your hand. Hook the slotted side onto a spoke to hold the tire in place. This frees both hands for the rest of the work.

Take a second lever and, once more, work the tip underneath the tire bead, about a few inches from the first lever. (Photo E.) Again, push down on your lever, to pop the bead away from its seat in the rim. If you can't do this, move your lever a half inch closer to the first lever. Continue to work the bead away from the rim all around the wheel, until you have one complete side of the tire free. Then, using your spoon from the opposite side of the wheel, work the second bead off the rim. (Photo F.) (You are now working the bead off the rim *away* from you in direction, as of course both beads must come off the same side to free the tire.) Taking one side of the tire off at a time is much easier than trying to force both beads at once. (Expect a new tire to be more difficult to remove than an old one.)

3. Remove the tube from the tire, checking both the outside and the inside of the tire for embedded glass, thorns, etc. (Photo G.) When you're sure that it's clean, move on to the tube. I've had only two holes in my life that leaked so

. G.

little that I was forced to hold them under water to look for air bubbles. All the other times I merely pumped up the tube and listened for escaping air. (If your tube has a Schrader valve, be sure the air is not escaping from the threaded center valve core. If this core is not screwed tightly into these threads, an air leak will result. The proper tool to tighten a valve core is the valve cover tool, a tiny slotted

H.

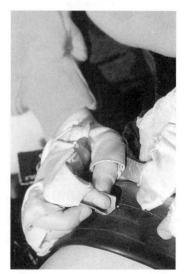

I.

metal cap that you should buy to replace the worthless black plastic caps present on all tubes sold. If you have a very slow leak, check that your valve core is tight before you remove the wheel from the frame. I've had this problem only once, but it's still worth checking.)

J.

K.

L.

When the hole is located, rough up the area with the patch kit (Photo H.) scraper. Be sure to do a good job of it, short of putting additional holes in the tube, and be sure to roughen an area a bit larger than the size of the patch. (Photo I.)

Apply the glue (unless you're using the new glueless patches), a bit more than necessary to cover the patch area. (Photos J. and K.) Most kits suggest waiting until the glue is dry to apply the patch. Hurry this step and there's a good chance you'll be taking the wheel off the bike again a few miles down the road. Be careful not to touch the patch side that goes on the tube, (Photo L.) and once in place press the edges of the patch with a tire spoon.

M.

N.

O.

4. When the patch appears to beholding well along the edges, pump a very slight amount of air into the tube to avoid wrinkles when it's placed back inside the tire. (Photo M.) Put the tube in the tire, then push the valve stem through the valve stem hole in the rim, and reseat one of the beads. Once one side of the tire—one bead—is back in place, begin reseating the second bead. (Photo N.) (Removing all air at this point reduces the chance of puncture.) In taking off a tire, begin *opposite* the stem; in replacing it, begin work at the stem and work away from it in both directions, being sure to keep the stem pointing straight up. Riders who fail to do this, or who ride with too little air pressure in their tires (which causes the tube to shift and the valve stem to angle out of the hole), cause wearing of the stem along its side and base. Once a hole occurs in the valve stem, the entire tube is shot; stems can't hold a patch.

You'll probably be able to reseat all but about six inches of the beads without tools. At this point use your tire spoon in the opposite manner from before—beveled end down. (Photo O.)

If both beads are properly seated and the stem is still perpendicular, inflate the tire to its desired pressure. Do this before you put the wheel back on the bike; it will mean less to mess with if you've goofed with the patch.

If the tire remains hard for a minute, replace the wheel, tighten axle nuts or the quick-release, reengage the chain if it's the rear wheel, *and* reset your brakes.

Freewheel Removal and Cleaning

Removal is an unfortunate necessity if a rear wheel spoke breaks on the freewheel side (which is almost the *only* place they break, due to the "dishing"; the flatter freewheel side's spokes are lesser-angled and therefore under greater pressure). First, determine which kind of freewheel you have and obtain the necessary tools. These will be:

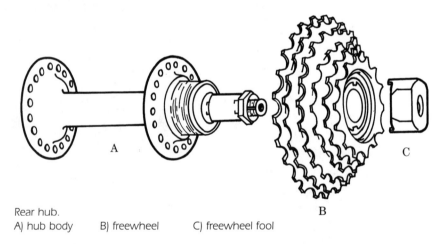

Rear hub.
A) hub body   B) freewheel   C) freewheel fool

On old-style freewheels—a freewheel-removal tool and vise (or large crescent or pipe wrench, or pocket vise if on the road).

On nonhyperglide cassette freewheels—two freewheel sprocket tools (also called chain whips) or, on the road, a cassette cracker, described by the manufacturer as "a mini-whip tool for on-the-road disassembly of rear hub cassettes." I've used one only twice, and it took a minute to follow the directions properly, but both times it worked beautifully.

On hyperglide cassette freewheels—a freewheel-removal tool and vise (or medium-sized crescent or pipe wrench, or pocket vise if on the road), or freewheel-removal tool and one chain whip.

Confused? Well, don't be; just concentrate on your particular system and forget the rest.

Remove the rear wheel, and unscrew and remove the quick-release mechanism. With the Shimano cassette-type freewheel, follow the directions provided by them in their Freehubs service instruction. (Cassette crackers come with a small instruction sheet for on-the-trail cog removal; follow the directions carefully.) With all other freewheels, slide the thin shaft of the quick-release through the pocket vise, the freewheel tool and the freewheel. Center the two prongs of the pocket vise over the handlebar stem, engage the flat sides of the freewheel tool (with the wheel above it), take hold of the wheel at the three and nine o'clock positions, and turn counterclockwise. If you're a strong rider, and if the freewheel hasn't been off the wheel before, you'll have to work at getting it off. Once removed, the spoke heads are visible and replacement can begin.

During those long years before the pocket vise (and now the cassette cracker for freehub assemblies) was invented, I struggled with other methods of "breaking" the freewheel. The easiest is finding a regular vise at a home or garage; the freewheel tool then is set into the vise jaws with its splined or notched teeth pointing up, and the wheel is simply fitted over it and turned (counterclockwise) free. A second relatively easy method is to locate a huge crescent or pipe wrench, place the tire standing up in front of you with the freewheel on the right side, engage the freewheel tool into both the freewheel and wrench, and press *downward*.

The hardest of all removals is with the seven-inch channel locks taking the place of a larger wrench, a shock cord wrapped around its handles to hold it together and provide the hand some sort of protection. I've done this only once, when there was no alternative, and it took its toll on both the tool and me. Buy a pocket vise or a cassette freewheel.

But what if you haven't a quick-release wheel? I've solved this problem for use with my mountain bike wheels and their large axles by drilling out the tiny hole in the pocket vise sufficiently to accept the axle, and then balancing the wheel and freewheel tool in place over the pocket vise. It's a bit less stable, but it works.

When it comes to cleaning a freewheel, the body (or core) can be disassembled, but you should do this only if you make watches for a living. My alternative is to set the freewheel upside down (smallest sprocket to the ground) on many sheets of folded newspaper. Now flush the core with Liquid Wrench. This is done by shooting the liquid between the dust ring and main body of the core—just inside the sprocket on the back side. Give the Liquid Wrench a few minutes to work through the bearings. Spin the freewheel several times and move it to a dry piece of paper, then flush again. If the ball bearings inside the core were dirty, the first newspaper will be dark with grease. A third flushing may be necessary; each time the newspaper should be left cleaner. Allow the bearings to dry for a few minutes, then apply a fine, light bicycle oil.

Spoke Replacement/Wheel Alignment

Let's begin with an analysis of the thin, spindly spoke. If you've never thought of it, ponder for a moment how such slender pillars of metal can hold up the weight of a bike, rider, and gear, while being light enough to spin almost effortlessly in circles around a hub. Now look closely at it: a

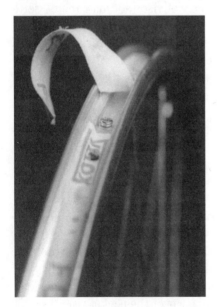

Rim tape removed, slotted (for screw-driver) spoke nipple shown.

Spoke pattern.

long shank, threads at the top where it screws into the nipple (protruding through the rim hole and holding the spoke in place and under desired tension), and at the other end a right-angle crook that holds it in the hub. That sharp bend is the danger point, the spoke's Achilles' heel.

More common, however, is a spoke that simply needs adjustment to help realign (make true again) a wheel. Wheels can be out of true in two ways: They can sway from side to side, and they can have high and low spots, a condition referred to as being out of round. Look closely at your wheel. Notice that the spokes reach out to the rim from both sides of the hub. Focus upon one spoke and think what tightening (shortening the length of) that single spoke will do. The rim will be pulled in two directions at the same time when the spoke is tightened, or moved back in two directions if loosened. Tighten the spoke and the rim will be (1) pulled closer to the hub, and (2) pulled in the direction of the side of the hub to which the other end of the spoke is attached. Loosen the spoke and the opposite movement will occur. Tighten a spoke that comes from the other side of the hub and the rim will move in that direction.

Trueing a wheel is most quickly and successfully accomplished with the wheel off the bike, the tire, tube, and rim tape removed, and with the assistance of a trueing stand. Such stands have small moveable metal indicators that you slide ever closer to the rim from both sides as the spoke adjustments bring the wheel increasingly into alignment. This can also be done without a stand, using the bike itself to hold the wheel and your thumb in place of the metal slides. In fact, since spokes break while riding, and because wheels become untrue when being used, chances are you'll do this while far from home.

Let's imagine you've broken a spoke on the rear wheel. Begin the repair by flipping your bike on its back and removing the wheel, tire, tube, and rim tape. If the break is on the freewheel side, remove the freewheel. (If you have a cassette freewheel you may prefer to use a cassette cracker or freewheel cog removal tools to spin off the first sprocket, disengage the three long metal rods running through the remaining cogs, and then lift off these cogs so as to reach the spoke/hub attachment points.) Put the wheel back on the bike without tightening axle nuts or the quick-release lever. (The spoke can be replaced with the wheel off the bike, but I find it much easier to work with when the wheel is back in place.)

Remove the broken spoke. This is easy; spokes break at the bevel, and

Rear wheel hub with broken spoke.

can be taken out by pulling from the nipple end. Take the nipple from the new spoke (the proper length of which you've determined long before by taking your wheel to the bike shop, or by measuring *very* carefully with a spoke rule). Look at the rear hub, and concentrate on the next closest spokes to the one that broke. If you see two spoke heads next to the empty hole in the hub, you know that your new spoke must enter from the other side, to follow the alternating pattern around the entire hub. Guide the spoke into the hole. (Don't be afraid to bend the spoke a bit.) Once it's completely through, look at the next closest spoke that enters the hub in the same direction as your replacement spoke. This will be your guide on lacing your replacement—how many spokes you must cross, and which to go over or under with the new spoke. (You'll have to bend the spoke even more here; be sure to bend it along its entire length, thereby not putting a crimp in it.)

Put the nipple into the rim, and thread the new spoke into it. Tighten the spoke until it is approximately the same tension as the rest, and then align the wheel (following the procedure below).

I prefer to align wheels with tire, tube, and rim tape removed. This allows for more accurate trueing, and exposes the screw head of the spoke nipple for adjustment with a screwdriver (necessary if you've rounded the nipple with the spoke wrench). It also allows you to *see* if too much spoke extends through the nipple head, in which case the metal file blade of the Swiss Army knife can be used to shorten it. (If you've purchased spare spokes of the proper length, you won't have a protrusion.) Restore your freewheel to its proper location, and replace your wheel in the frame (if it isn't already there) as it will be when you ride. Tighten axle nuts or close the quick-release lever, but keep the brakes free. Standing behind your wheel, with the bike still on its back, spin the wheel with your hand and note the wobble (movement side to side).

Determine the extent of the wobble by placing your thumb next to the wheel rim (with the palm of your hand resting on the chainstay), so that your thumbnail lightly touches the rim at every point except for the wobble. At that point the rim will reach out and smack your thumbnail; your job is to pull that wobble back into line with the rest of the rim.

Check the tension of the spokes in the area of the wobble. Chances are they'll be a bit looser than the rest of the spokes in the wheel. Tighten the spoke at the center of the wobble—just a bit at a time, watching its effect upon the rim—then move on to the spokes on either side. (Read the next two paragraphs before proceeding.)

Tightening a spoke with a spoke wrench.

But how much do you tighten a spoke? And what if two spokes appear to sit right smack in the middle of the problem area? Easy. Just recall that spokes reach out to the rim from both sides of the hub. Naturally, tightening a spoke coming from the right side pulls the rim toward the right; if from the left hub side it pulls to the left. If your wobble is to the right, you'll be tightening the spokes that come from the left side of the hub. I always start off with a slight adjustment—about a half turn for the spoke at wobble center, a quarter turn for spokes on either side, a one-eighth turn for the next two spokes.

On occasion you might have to loosen some spokes and tighten others in the wobble area to produce a true wheel, especially if you've trued your wheel several times before. In loosening spokes, follow the same pattern as above; more toward wobble center, less thereafter.

When your thumbnail-guide tells you all is well, you have two final things to do. First, check your spokes for approximately the same tension on all. You won't be perfect on this, but at least be close or you'll be aligning your wheel again soon. Second, step to the side of your bike, spin the wheel, and check for its "round." If you have one high spot, tighten the spokes slightly in this area—to pull the rim toward the hub a bit. But be sure to watch that you don't lose your side-to-side true as you do this.

Let me add that I find wheel alignment to be the most delicate, and thus the most difficult, repair on a bike. Go easy at first, and try to be patient. Your spokes will appreciate it.

Cone Adjustments/Wheel Bearing Maintenance

Most cyclists are seldom out on tour so long as to require wheel bearing service, and thus do not have to carry cone wrenches. (Cones are the threaded, cone-shaped pieces named for the tapering end that rests against the bearings; the other end is squared off to fit the wrench used to adjust pressure against the bearings.) Most of these mechanisms today are sealed, thus requiring no maintenance, and under normal conditions you needn't give your cones a thought on a backcountry tour. However, I pack the thin cone wrenches so that I can make the proper adjustments should anything go wrong on any of my rides, and of course when I pull full bearing maintenance during winter cross-country road tours.

Cone wrench.

Should you decide to readjust your cone bearing pressure, hold the locknut on one side of the hub (see photo) with a crescent wrench or channel locks, and use a second wrench to loosen the locknut on the opposite hub side. Unscrew the locknut completely, putting it someplace where you won't kick it as you continue working. Next, remove the keyed lock washer ("keyed" refers to the small pointed flange of metal on the inside of the washer, which fits the groove on the axle). Now you can hold the locknut on the opposite hub side immobile, while very carefully adjusting cone pressure against the bearings on the dismantled side. As with so many adjustments on a bike, you are looking for that perfect point that allows free rotation of the wheel, but no lateral sway.

When I want to inspect or service (lube or replace) wheel bearings, I usually remove the locknut, keyed washer, and cone on one side of the axle only, and then carefully slide the axle out of the hub while watching for bearings that might fall out. In this manner I must rebuild only one side of the axle during reassembly.

The next task is getting past the seals. Most can be removed with the very thin blade of a knife, but you must take great care that they are not bent in the process. Just slip the blade in under the seal in various places around its perimeter and pry free. (If this has you concerned, inquire at the best shop in your region for the special tool made for seal removal.)

Knife blade beneath rear wheel seal.

Use the flat edge of your screwdriver to remove the bearings, but not until you've noticed two things—the very small gap that exists when all the bearings are present (they should not be wedged in tightly) and exactly how many bearings there are. If some bearings have fallen free when the axle was removed, just count those and the bearings still in place and divide by two. You will then have the number you should replace on either side.

Now remove all the bearings, cleaning and inspecting each individually for pitting and cracks. Remember that bearings cost almost nothing compared to a hub; if you save a few cents by hanging on to worn-out bearings, it will cost you a new hub in the end.

Bearing sizes generally fall into the following categories, but take one with you to the bike shop to make sure you buy proper replacements:

$^3/_{16}$"—front hub

$^1/_4$"—rear hub, bottom bracket

$^1/_8$"—freewheel

$^5/_{32}$"—pedal, headset

Once all bearings are removed and cleaned, wipe all grease out of the bearing races (the circular housing for the ball bearings). You are now ready to begin rebuilding the wheel.

Apply a bead of fresh grease to the bearing cup (race) of one side of the hub. Replace the bearings, then cover each with a second bead of grease. Replace the seal by laying it in place, then tapping lightly with the handle of your six-inch crescent wrench.

Take the axle (which still has the cone, lock washer, and locknut on one side) and insert it into the hub side in which you have just replaced the bearings. Be sure to clean and check the cones for pitting as well. Now you can turn your wheel over and replace the bearings in the other side; the seal and cone will keep the bearings on the reverse side from falling out.

Once the bearings are in place around the axle on this second side, replace the seal, then thread the cone into place against the bearings only finger tight. Slide on the lock washer and screw on the locknut. Your hub is now rebuilt, but not ready to be ridden; you still need to adjust the cones to the proper pressure against the bearings. Too loose, and the wheel will roll from side to side, in time ruining your bearings and cone and cup. Too tight, and the wheel will not roll easily.

Use the cone wrench to back off the cones a quarter turn or less if, when you turn the axle, it doesn't revolve easily in the hub. (The wheel is still off the bike; you should be checking its revolution by hand.) What usually happens is that a person will back off the cones too far, creating side play. This is when the axle moves back and forth in the hub. Even a slight amount of movement will be greatly accentuated when the wheel is replaced on the frame, so try to remove the side play while still retaining free rolling movement of the axle.

Just when you think you've got the best of both worlds, tighten the locknuts on both sides. (Hold one side fast, with a crescent wrench or in a vise, while tightening the other side.) The first time you do this you'll notice that you've tightened the cone somewhat by snugging the locknuts—and you'll have to readjust the cone once more. Merely hold the locknut on one side of the axle with your crescent wrench, while backing off the same-side cone ever so slightly with the cone wrench. This is usually sufficient to align it properly, but if not, back off the locknut a quarter turn and try again. Expect it to be difficult at first, and much easier the second time.

When side play is absent and the axle moves freely, replace the axle washers and nuts (or quick-release mechanism) and restore the wheel to the frame. Once it is secured, spin the wheel and check again for rolling ease and for side play. If it's not correct, don't sell your bicycle; you'll have to adjust the cones once more. But don't give up.

Freewheel Disassembly

Friction produced by the meeting of the metal chain and metal freewheel sprocket teeth will eventually wear them away so badly that they require replacement. The life of a sprocket can be extended greatly by correct alignment when changing gears; that is, train your ear to hear the noise produced when you haven't shifted the chain exactly over the cog. When you are way off center (sometimes spoken of as being between gears) the clatter is unmistakable, but damage is being done even when the misalignment (and resultant noise) is much reduced but still present.

Sprocket life is also shortened by cross-chaining—a reference to the visual appearance when one's chain is forced onto the largest chain ring and largest freewheel sprocket, or conversely upon the smallest chain ring and smallest freewheel sprocket. Looking at either of these conditions from above shows the chain reaching at an awkward angle from the far inside of the chain rings to the far outside of the freewheel, or vice versa. In both instances the chain is stretched across the widths of chain ring and freewheel, the angled metal edges eating away at chain links and sprocket teeth.

Proper shifting will give you very long sprocket life, but at some point one or two of them (those sprockets you use most often and usually the smallest two) will let you know they're getting old. Your chain will skip under pressure, a condition reversible only by sprocket replacement (and often requiring a replacement of the chain at the same time). Some riders erroneously believe they need a new freewheel at this time, a needless and costly response. Simply invest in a couple of sprocket tools (which you'll need anyway for alternating gear ratios, should you ever become interested in doing so), head to the shop for new sprockets (with the necessary information of type of freewheel and exact number of teeth), and learn the following repair procedure.

Because most of us don't have large workroom vises, I'll describe the procedure of leaving the freewheel on the wheel and using two sprocket tools. If you do have a vise, place a slat of wood on either vise face to grip the largest sprocket, and close tightly. This in effect serves the purpose of

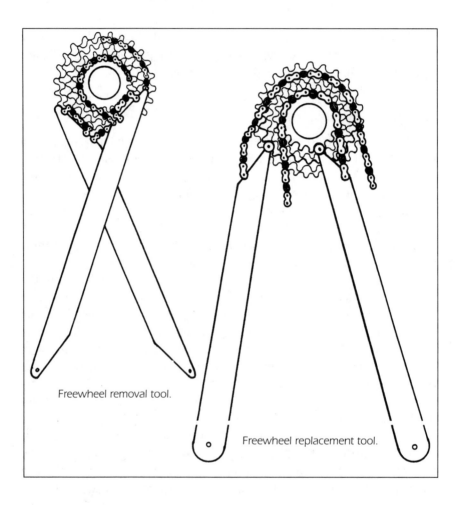

Freewheel removal tool.

Freewheel replacement tool.

a second sprocket tool. There are also commercial sprocket holders (free-wheel-axle vise tools) that take the place of the wood blocks and hold the cluster (freewheel) in a horizontal position for the easiest of all disassemblies.

When using two sprocket tools, place the chain of one tool around the second-to-largest sprocket, wrapping the chain in a clockwise direction. Notice that the tools have a device (on the same rod end as the chain, but opposite side) to engage the sprocket and hold fast between the teeth; this device should be engaged and pointed in the direction you want to turn that particular sprocket. (Another type of sprocket tool has a shorter piece of chain in place of the rivet tip, in addition to the longer-length chain. The grip is more secure, and the handles are crossed and pushed toward one another for disassembly. Follow the directions that come with these tools, and expect the drawings to be somewhat confusing at first.)

In the opposite direction, wrap the chain of the second tool around the first (smallest) cog. Place these tools so that the handles are only a few inches apart. This allows greater control, because the handles must be pushed toward one another to unscrew the top sprocket. A strong rider's freewheel will require a great deal of strength to disassemble; the first two sprockets are actually tightened on the freewheel body during pedaling. (When you use two sprocket tools, be very careful not to apply uneven pressure against the handles. This will cause the entire freewheel to tilt and your tools will slip off. No real problem, but it does propel your knuckles into the sprocket teeth.)

On most freewheels the first two sprockets screw off the freewheel body or core in a counterclockwise direction, and the remaining cogwheels lift off. These most often have small lugs that fit the notches in the core, and usually have spacer rings between them or built into one or the other side of the sprocket. Don't get the sequence mixed up when you take things apart (I lay out each piece on newspaper as it comes off). Also, you *must* replace the sprockets with the same side up as you found them. If you drop one or get confused, study the bevel on the remaining cogs and match the errant sprocket accordingly.

Shimano cassette-type freewheels are broken down somewhat differently. The first sprocket or two will be removed in the same manner, but after that you will find several long, very thin bolts that reach through the inside perimeter of the remaining sprockets. Hold the top end of the bolt with a wrench, then reach around to the bottom with a second and unscrew the holding nuts. Now simply lift each sprocket free.

▪ DERAILLEURS ▪

Derailleurs have improved greatly in performance since the birth of mountain bikes, have been sealed amazingly well to the elements, and remain—even with the addition of click shifting—wonderfully simple to adjust. Interestingly, technology has come full circle since my first tour more than thirty years ago; among the many types of shifters now available are the increasingly popular "twist-grips" offered by Grip Shift. The number of speeds available has risen miraculously from three to twenty-four today. And yet, despite the simplicity of on-the-road adjustments of these new changers (an old term for derailleurs), most recreational riders endure slipping gears until they make it to a bike shop.

It needn't be so. The following pages and pictures plus the instruction sheets and mechanical drawings in the appendix, are designed first to provide an understanding of these excellent mechanisms, and next to embolden you to take them in hand. An hour is all that's required to make sloppy shifting, and fear of transmission breakdown, a thing of the past.

Rear derailleur.

Derailleur is from the French and means "to take from the rails"; in cycling it refers to the movement of the chain from one sprocket to another. This is accomplished through a series of shifters, gear cables, and front and rear derailleurs.

Basically, a gear cable runs from the shifter (which today includes thumb, twist, and trigger shifters) along the down tube and chainstay, or the top tube and seatstay, through a cable-adjusting barrel (similar in principle to that found on brakes), to a cable anchor bolt on the changer. When you activate the shifter (pushing the large thumb shifter away from you, for instance) you tighten the cable, which causes the derailleur to lift the chain from a smaller sprocket and set it upon a larger one. Naturally, there are limits to how far in either direction you would want your chain to go; this limitation is established by "high-" and "low-" gear adjusting screws. The high-gear screw on rear derailleurs keeps the chain from moving beyond the smallest sprocket and falling off the freewheel; the low-gear screw keeps the chain from moving beyond the largest sprocket and attacking your spokes. The third screw present on some rear changers is an angle screw. Its task is to move the derailleur body so that the upper pulley is at an optimum position below the freewheel for transporting the chain.

Below the derailleur housing are two pulleys, or rollers. Notice that the chain rolls over one and under the second. The top pulley is the jockey, or guide, pulley, named for its task of jockeying the chain into place over a sprocket. The bottom one is the tension pulley; it takes up the slack in the chain when the derailleur moves from a larger to a smaller sprocket. The final thing you should notice are the points of lubrication (seen now only in older, nonsealed changers)—small holes in the derailleur body that run toward the internal springs. If these springs can be seen, apply a couple of drops of lubricant each month (use one of those with a nonpetroleum base if your bike is often in dirt or sand), and wipe off the excess.

Derailleur Adjustment

Before doing anything, give your bike a thorough visual inspection. The most common adjustment problems on ATBs are bent derailleurs, bent derailleur hangers (a hanger is the metal plate that attaches the changer to the bike), and stretched cables. If none of these obvious difficulties is present, you will have to move on to more delicate procedures. Both inspection and adjustment, by the way, are made easier by placing the bike in a bike stand, or by otherwise raising the rear wheel from the ground to facilitate shifting through the gears.

Let's begin with the headache of bent rear derailleurs and hangers. The most common causes of this particular malady are: (1) dropping or crashing the bike on the derailleur side (yes, learning to crash only onto your left—the nonderailleur side—is difficult, but *try!*); and (2) shifting the derailleur into the spokes because of improper derailleur adjustment. An easy way to check for alignment is to kneel behind your rear wheel, with your eye at derailleur level to sight down the drivetrain. The derailleur hanger and derailleur pulley cage should be parallel to one another, and also to the plane of the frame and wheels. Check this in the most inboard (lowest) and outboard (highest) gear combinations. Look to see if the derailleur pulley cage is brushing against the spokes in the inboard gear combination. As a final check, grasp the derailleur at the lower pulley and gently wiggle it back and forth, without disturbing the upper portion of the derailleur (the body of the changer, above the upper pulley). A small amount of lateral play is normal, but a worn derailleur will feel loose and will travel laterally a quarter or a half inch at the lower pulley. This can be a cause of erratic shifting.

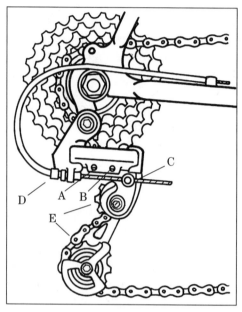

Rear derailleur

Set screws for rear derailleur (notice "L" and "H" for low and high).

A) low gear adjusting screw
B) high gear adjusting screw
C) cable anchor bolt
D) adjusting barrel
E) pulleys

Don't despair if your inspection reveals a bent derailleur hanger, for you might still be in luck; that is, if your hanger is made of steel and if it's not cracked. Run through the following steps. First, remove the derailleur and affix the jaws of a large adjustable wrench to the hanger. Now, *carefully,* bend the hanger back into line with the rest of the dropout. Try to get it right the first time; excessive tweaking will fatigue the steel and have you hitching a ride to the bike shop for a replacement. Which it might have, if it's a shop that's been around awhile. If not, you can ask them to order one for you, though chances are they'll suggest the alternative of buying one behind the counter that's attached to a brand-new derailleur.

Now, if you bent your derailleur in such a manner as to oval or strip the threads in your hanger, but the hanger isn't bent or if it was bent but you've restored it, take heart. Most bike shops can tap or helicoil the hole to restore the threads.

And if your bent derailleur hanger is aluminum? Well, the downside is that unlike steel hangers, aluminum hangers should not be straightened. This is because the metal is too brittle, and if it doesn't crack off when you lay into it with your large adjustable wrench, it probably will fall off just as soon as you are the farthest possible distance from your car on the next ride. The upside, however, is that most bike manufacturers offer bolt-on replacement hangers for their aluminum frames.

Rear derailleurs that are bent slightly but which have no broken parts can often be restored to their proper alignment. Leave them on the bike, and with your hands or adjustable pliers, straighten the derailleur until it appears aligned from all directions. If you aren't sure how much force to use or what the proper alignment is, have a competent mechanic show you. For derailleurs that have been shifted into the spokes, be sure to check the chain to see if any of the links have been twisted. Twisted chains will cause skipping or unusual noises when the bike is pedaled. Replace the twisted links, or the entire chain.

If you've purchased your bike in the past six or seven years, there is a good chance that it is outfitted with click shifting (or index shifting). You should be warned that click shift systems are more sensitive to dirt, grime, and cable friction than are the old, simple, and wonderfully reliable friction shift systems. This is, by the way, the reason that I made sure the click shift shifters on my newest bike had a friction-option setting. I refuse to allow my riding time, and especially my touring, to be affected by temperamental mechanical systems—particularly when they are unnecessary. And so the third time I had to dial in a recorrection I switched the derailleur to friction and said goodbye to clicking forever.

Clicking instantly into the proper gear might be of great importance to racers, but for the rest of us I honestly can't see the reason for this extra mechanical hassle. And besides, friction shifting allows the rider to feel the increasing tension upon the cable, the flex of the derailleur body, the movement of the jockey pulley, and the chain settling into place onto another cog.

Before you make any adjustment to your derailleur, clean away the accumulated grime on your chain, chain rings (the front cogs), rear cogs, and rear derailleur pulleys. The pulleys should spin freely. (Note: The upper and lower pulleys on Shimano rear derailleurs are different, so be careful not to mix them up when you remove them for cleaning.) If it is necessary to remove the cable to facilitate this cleaning, see the upcoming section on cable replacement.

Let's say your rear derailleur is both clean and aligned, but that you're still experiencing problems in shifting. Such problems usually fall into two categories. (1) On all types of shifting systems, the chain won't shift up onto the largest rear cog or overshifts off the largest rear cog into the spokes. Similarly, but at the other end of the freewheel, the chain won't shift down onto the smallest rear cog or overshifts into the frame. (2) The second category of usual rear derailleur problems concerns click shift systems, and in this instance the shifting is erratic when choosing cogs between the smallest and largest sprockets in your freewheel. That is, the chain jumps or skips to adjacent cogs, or the chain hesitates when shifting, or the chain makes noise because it is not centered on the chosen cog.

Now, the first category of shifting problems above is the same for both friction and click shifting systems, and is due to misadjustment of the high (often marked *H* on the derailleur body) and/or low (*L*) limit (or limiting) screws. Let's say your chain can't quite make it up onto the largest sprocket of the freewheel. Recalling that the larger freewheel sprockets provide the lower (easier to pedal) gears, simply turn counterclockwise the L screw of the rear derailleur—a quarter to a half turn to start. If your chain falls off the smallest sprocket (highest gear) of your freewheel, turn the H screw on the rear derailleur clockwise—thereby limiting the chain's movement away from the freewheel.

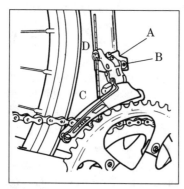

Front derailleur

A) low gear adjusting screw
C) cage
B) high gear adjusting screw
D) cable anchor bolt

Front derailleur set screws.

Similar problems with the chain rings can be solved through the adjustment of the front derailleur limiting screws. Look closely inside the derailleur housing and, with some, you'll actually be able to see these limiting screws making contact with the body.

But let's return to the problem of the chain not quite reaching up onto the largest freewheel sprocket. You've adjusted the L screw, can in fact see that the housing is not making contact with the limiting screw, and yet the chain can't quite fall into place. In such a case (very infrequent), the problem is not with the derailleur but with the cable. It has stretched over time, and now must be readjusted. Most recent bikes have gear-cable adjustment barrels to remove this slack quickly and easily (as with the brake-cable adjustment systems); if yours does not, shift onto the smallest freewheel sprocket, then loosen the cable-fixing (or anchor) bolt (which clamps the cable into place on the derailleur housing), shorten the cable slightly, and then retighten the anchor bolt.

The second category of shifting problems is due to improper cable tension on click shift systems. The diagram shows how to correct this problem by turning the cable-adjusting barrel on the rear derailleur. However, be careful not to back the barrel (that is, not to turn it counterclockwise) completely out of the derailleur; too many turns can make it bend or break off. If the barrel needs more than three complete turns, the cable has too much slack in it. In this case, first turn the barrel clockwise until it stops against the derailleur, then remove the excessive slack by resetting the cable at the cable anchor bolt. Any further adjustments can be done with the barrel. If the barrel is too difficult to turn by hand, loosen the cable clamp to release cable tension at the barrel and lubricate the threads on the barrel. Turn the barrel in and out several times to free it.

And now to front derailleurs. The two most common shifting problems here, with derailleurs that are not damaged, are (1) the chain rubs against the sides of the derailleur, and (2) the chain overshifts off the inner or outer chain rings or won't make the shift onto a chain ring.

In the first instance, the problem is usually caused by improper alignment of the front derailleur, or by bent chain rings that might require replacement. Consult the section above on rear derailleur alignment, or the appropriate diagram, to bring about proper alignment. (In some instances the outer front derailleur cage may have to be aligned parallel to the chain line instead of the chain ring, if rubbing still occurs in the outer—highest—gear combination. This can be done by loosening the derailleur clamp on the seat tube just enough to rotate the derailleur but not enough to allow the cable tension to pull it down onto the outer chain ring. If rubbing occurs because the derailleur can't shift in or out any farther, the problem is the misadjustment of the limiting screws.)

In the case of overshifting in either direction, you'll have to have at your high- and low-gear limiting screws. Just go through the same process as described above with rear derailleurs. And also as with the rear derailleur, it may be necessary to loosen the cable anchor bolt and reset the cable to allow the derailleur the freedom to move to the new limit settings. In a few rare cases, the chain won't shift into the most inboard (lowest) gear combination even though the low-gear limit screw has been backed out (turned counterclockwise) all the way. If inspection shows that a part of the front derailleur is in contact with the seat tube, the only remedy will be to install a longer bottom bracket axle to move the crankset away from the frame. A few millimeters of clearance is usually all that is required.

Cable Replacement

Back when all my riding was done on thin-tire touring bikes, I broke, on average, one or two derailleur cables a year. These were, of course, rear cables: Rear derailleurs see so much more use than do front changers. These days, however, when all of my many thousands of annual miles are put on mountain bikes, I can say I've never, ever, broken a cable—front or rear—on a mountain bike.

You'll understand why when you compare bikes: ATB cables look like they belong on motorcycles. When bike shop mechanics do see mountain bike cable breaks, they are generally the result of one of two problems: (1) The cable anchor bolt has chewed up the cable, and individual metal strands begin breaking or fraying backwards. (2) Moisture creates rust on a portion of the cable inside the cable housing (the black or other-color plastic sheath inside which the metal cable runs) and jams cable movement. The cable housing on click shift systems can also affect shifting if it has any kinks, breaks, or missing end caps.

Very rarely do ATB cables break at the shift lever, as they do on road bikes. But there is one great similarity, one that has required me to replace cable on both thin- and fat-tire bikes, though not because of breaks. This is my occasional failure to crimp an end cap (the tiny metal sleeve that slips over the cut end of a cable to prevent it from fraying) sufficiently to hold it in place. When it comes time to remove the cable for lubrication (usually twice a year, when I'm servicing my bearings), the fraying prevents me from pushing it through the housing once again, and a complete replacement is required.

Begin this process by loosening the cable-fixing bolt of whichever derailleur is affected by the broken cable. Remove the cable—but only after taking careful note of the cable position on its final path around the derailleur housing blocks to the fixing bolt. If the rear derailleur is involved, screw the cable-adjusting barrel clockwise—into the derailleur body—until it stops, and then back it out one full turn. This will give the adjusting barrel the freedom to be adjusted in either direction once the cable has been anchored. If your shifter has a brakelike cable-adjusting barrel on it (similar to that found near the derailleur body), screw it in until it is flush with the shifter body. Place the shifter in its most relaxed (no tension being applied to the cable) position. Feed the noncyclinder end of the new cable through the cable housing (I've always used grease or oil when doing this; mechanic friends tell me they prefer to spray Tri-Flow into the housing, and that Shimano recommends using no oil whatsoever inside the housing on its index-shift bikes), then through the cable-adjusting barrel (if present), and on to the cable-fixing bolt. Note: Some mountain bike shift levers require that they be shifted one or two positions to allow a proper angle for cable insertion through the shifter housing. Also, on some shifters, a small cover piece may have to be removed to insert the cable into the shifter body. Grip Shift's Service Instructions illustrate one such cover, and will take you step by step through its more involved replacement procedures. Trigger shifters should be relatively simple to deal with once you've read and understood the material in this chapter.

When replacing a rear derailleur cable, pull the cable slightly taut (not so much that the derailleur body moves) and secure it by tightening the cable-fixing bolt, but only after stretching it somewhat (as indicated on the instruction sheets). The rear derailleur pulleys should be in line with the smallest freewheel sprocket at this point. If they are not, turn the high-gear (H) adjusting screw until that line is attained; if it cannot be reached with the adjusting screw, it means you have pulled the cable too tight. Loosen the cable anchor bolt and readjust the cable tension.

To make the low gear adjustment, first be sure that cable stretch is not the reason for the derailleur's failure to reach the largest sprockets. If this is not the problem, carefully shift the chain onto the largest freewheel sprocket;

INSTALLATION

Grip Shify Actuator

7/8" Plastic Washer

Handlebar Grip

Clamping
Screw 3mm
Allen Key
Tighten to 17
in lbs

Cable

CABLE CHANGE

REAR

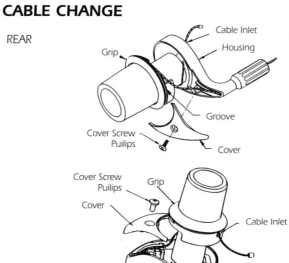

Cable Inlet

Housing

Grip

Groove

Cover Screw
Puilips

Cover

Cover Screw
Puilips

Grip

Cover

Cable Inlet

Spring

Housing

Cable Exit

FRONT

LUBRICATION

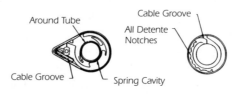

Around Tube

Cable Groove

All Detente
Notches

Cable Groove

Spring Cavity

Grip Shift service instruction

if this can't be done, turn the low-gear (L) adjusting screw counterclockwise until it can. As a final check, turn the low-gear adjusting screw clockwise—into the rear derailleur body—until you feel resistance.

When replacing a front derailleur cable, loosen the cable anchor bolt to allow for cable movement, then place the chain on the largest rear and smallest front sprockets. Then turn the low-gear (L) adjusting screw until there's a slight clearance between the chain and the inside plate of the chain cage (chain guide). If this can't be done, it means you've pulled the cable too taut; loosen the cable anchor bolt, correct the tension, and retighten.

Next, place the chain on the smallest rear and largest front sprockets. Then turn the high-gear (H) adjusting screw until there is a slight clearance between the chain and the outside plate of the chain cage. When these adjustments to the rear and front derailleurs have been made, switch the chain through all possible gear combinations. On many bikes it is normal for the shifting to be difficult or noisy in the gears where the chain line is the most extreme (i.e., when you're cross-chained, where you shouldn't be when pedaling; this is when your chain is wrapped around your largest front chain ring and largest rear cog, and on the smallest front chain ring and smallest rear cog).

As stated above, one method to eliminate cable friction is to lube the cable or the inside of the cable housing. Friction can also be reduced by replacing standard cables with those coated with Gore-Tex or Teflon. Cable friction is the main source of erratic shifting with the Light Action Shimano rear derailleurs when used with some non-Shimano shifters. This is because the Shimano derailleurs have less spring tension than do other brands.

And a few final suggestions. In the old days, when the derailleur was filthy, it was common to remove the entire component and swish it around in a coffee can of gasoline or other solvent. These days, however, when main pivot springs are sealed, such action hurts more than it helps. Also, don't use WD-40 to lubricate the inside of cable housings. WD-40 is an excellent solvent, but it's far too light to be counted on for long-term lubrication. Also, when replacing or upgrading drivetrain parts, be aware that the design of these parts and their compatibility change frequently—often within a calendar year. As an example, be sure that the number of rear cogs on your bike (in your freewheel) equals the number of shifts on the new rear shifter you've purchased. Also, be aware that derailleurs used on so-called compact or microdrive drivetrains don't work very well with "regular" drivetrains. If you're in doubt about compatibility, haul your entire bike into the shop when purchasing new parts.

▪ CHAIN ▪

Pavement cyclists have few problems with their chains. In fact, if they can train themselves to hear the awful squeaking of a dry chain begging for lubrication and then spend five minutes applying a bit of oil (a single drop on each roller), all will be well in their drivetrain world.

For mountain bikers who spend a lot of time in dirt and sand, however, it's a very different story. They *must* learn this part of their bike's anatomy, or suffer breakdowns. Occasional cleaning is essential; the kinds of lubricants available (liquid or spray petroleum bases, or nonpetroleum Teflons or paraffin) must be known, understood, and used.

Beyond this, mountain bikers have to be able to handle broken chains in the backcountry (by adding a replacement link, or at least shortening the chain; then avoid combinations of the largest chainwheels and sprockets and thereby be able to ride home) and to free a frozen link (much more common with ATBs than with pavement bikes) when one appears.

Frozen and Broken Links

When a link becomes frozen (a condition often caused by insufficient lubrication), it makes the problem known by jumping over teeth in the sprockets or by causing the rear derailleur to jerk forward suddenly as it passes over the jockey and tension pulleys. Elevate your rear wheel and turn the crank to find the culprit link; when you do, coat it with a light oil (if you are using oil as your lubrication, that is) and work the link side to side (the opposite direction of its normal movement) with your fingers. This may free it. If not, you'll have to employ the chain tool.

This tool, when viewed from the side, looks like a wide U, with two shorter walls of metal between. Place the tool in front of you with the handle to the right side. Twist the handle counterclockwise to remove the rivet pin from view. Now, take the chain and place it over the first of these inner walls from the right side. (It will usually be somewhat wider than the left-hand wall.) Notice, when you view your chain tool from the top, that these walls have an open space in the middle and that the chain roller rests in it

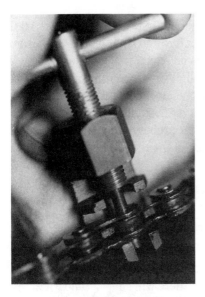

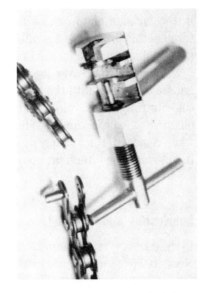

Chain rivet tool in action; notice rivet pin being pushed through the roller and side plate.

Chain tool with disconnected chain.

with the plates on either side of the wall. (Look at an individual link. Each is made up of these metal side plates, small round bars called rollers to engage the teeth of the sprockets, and tiny rivets to hold the side plates and rollers together.)

To free a frozen link, place it as described above on the right-hand wall of the chain rivet tool. Turn the tool handle clockwise until the tool rivet pin touches the chain rivet. As you turn the handle more, notice how the plates move slightly farther apart. Most often only the slightest rivet adjustment is necessary to free the link. Be sure not to push the chain rivet flush with the slide plate; its length is such that it should extend slightly past the plates on both sides. If it's necessary to push the rivet flush to free the link, simply turn the chain over in the tool and apply pressure against the opposite end of the rivet.

In the case of a chain break, a spare link and chain tool in your kit allows you to remove the broken link completely and replace it with a spare. This requires that the chain rivet be driven out of one side plate past the roller, yet still remain in place in the far side plate. (I know this sounds confusing, but it won't be when you're attempting the repair.) Keeping the rivet in the far side plate can be a little tricky at first, so I suggest you run through this procedure a couple of times before you try it on the trail. Bike shops will often have lengths of old chains on which you can practice.

Place the chain over the left-hand wall of your chain tool and turn the handle clockwise until the tool rivet pin touches the chain rivet. Then continue turning very carefully, until the roller can be pulled free, but with the chain rivet still in the far side plate. You'll probably find that it's frozen when replaced. If so, simply place this link on the right-hand plate and free it, following the directions above.

Lubrication and Cleaning

In the past few years a number of commercial brush-and-solvent-type chain cleaners have entered the market. If used often, these will do a fair job of removing the larger part of road grime. But there will come a time when the old procedure of complete chain removal, a good dunking in a coffee can of white gas (or other solvent), and frontal attack with a toothbrush is required. I then hang mine to drip dry, rub it with a cloth, clean all chain contact points on the bike (chainwheels, cogs, derailleur pulleys), and reinstall.

Because I'm most often on dirt and pavement (relatively seldom on sand), and because I prefer a small bottle of liquid oil in my pannier to an aerosol can, I choose against both paraffin and sprays for lubrication. My practice is simply to use a single drop of oil on each roller, spin the chain a few times, let it sit for awhile, then wipe almost dry with a cloth.

However, a friend who rides the sands of southern Utah quite often and another who rides primarily in dirt swear by paraffin. Their arguments are a cleaner bike and less wear and tear on the chain and all its contact points (which they attribute to dirt not being attracted to—and held in place by— an oily, greasy chain). Yet when I asked two mechanic friends in my former home of Salt Lake for their opinion of paraffin, their response was a single word: "Dinosaur."

I begged them to explain. They had tested paraffin's efficiency by adding oil to the paraffined chain of a bike they were pedaling on a tune-up stand. The cyclic rate increased dramatically. The mechanics agree that wax doesn't attract dirt, but Teflon-based lubricants that go to a dry rather than a wet finish, they say, are almost as good at repelling dirt and sand and yet do a better job of lubrication. *And* they're much easier to apply.

Chain Length

How long should your chain be? Long enough to do the job properly. Until only a few years ago there were two or three standard methods of determining chain length that seldom failed. My preference (simply because I could remember it) was the method that began with putting the chain on the largest sprockets, front and rear. This pulled the rear derailleur cage almost parallel with the chainstay. I would then give it a bit of assistance to make it taut, and try to lift the chain at the top of the chain ring. If I had between one-half and one full link of extra chain at this point, I was fine.

But today, due to index shifting and other developments, you must determine length by "derailleur-specific directions." In other words, consult your owner's manual. I still prefer the foolproof plan of riding a bike long enough to know that all works perfectly, then very carefully counting the number of links and writing it down in about a dozen places. Or, when you need a new chain, which you'll determine by lateral play of a half inch or so and the fact that no amount of lubricant will quiet it when pedaling, simply clean the old one carefully and haul it to the shop. Remember, *clean* it before you spread it out on the bike shop owner's counter.

▪ PEDALS ▪

So-called sealed pedals, 99 percent of the time, are only shielded. And because we're once again dealing with a part of the bike that can go for years without acting up, pedals are neglected. Chances are, therefore, that when you finally do get around to trying to locate that annoying click you hear when pedaling, you'll find very dry, very brown bearings.

Begin by removing the outer oval pedal-guard (not present on all models) with a very small Allen wrench. A larger Allen is then needed to remove the pedal spindle (axle) cap; on most there is simply a plastic dust cap that takes its place. (If the dust cap sits flush with the pedal body, it pries off; if it sits above it, it screws off. Usually.) This is as far as some people ever get with pedals, and that's farther than most. They unscrew or pry up the cap,

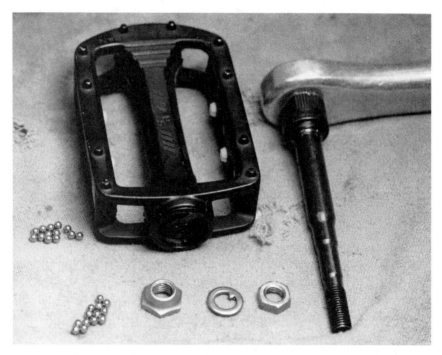

Pedal disassembled.

look in at the locknut, lock washer, cone, and bearings, squirt some grease inside, and replace the cap.

What they don't seem to know, or to care about, is that pedals have bearings on *both* sides of the pedal axle. So if this kind of quick and dirty maintenance appeals to you, at least pry off the back dust cap as well (the side closer to the crankarm) and give those bearings a drink. They'll appreciate it.

But if you really want to make your pedals happy, try removing first the locknut (easiest with a socket wrench, due to the pedal housing), then the lock washer, and then the cone. Some pedals have cones with serrated faces, to make unscrewing them an easy task with a screwdriver tip. Others require needle-nose pliers, or anything else (plus patience) that will reach deep into your pedal housing. Once free, the pedal body will slide off, granting access to the rear bearings.

This will be a snap if you've already worked on your wheel hubs. (It also seems easier to me if I leave the pedals attached to the bike crankarms when I'm pulling maintenance.) Clean and inspect as before, then rebuild

Model PD-M730

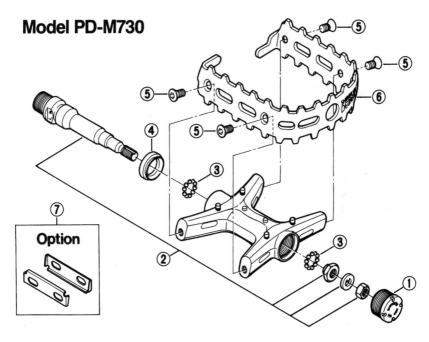

1) Cap
2) Pedal Axle Unit (Right /B.C. 9/16"x20T.P.I.)
   Pedal Axle Unit (Right /UNF1/2"x20T.P.I.)
   Pedal Axle Unit (Left /B.C. 9/16"x20T.P.I.)
   Pedal Axle Unit (Left /UNF1/2"x20T.P.I.)
3) Steel Ball (1/8" 10 pcs.

4) Seal
5) Plate Fixing Screw
6) Right Side Plate
   Left Side Plate
7) Toe-Clip Adapter (2 sets) Option

Courtesy Shimano (pedal diagram)

using a great deal of grease (any extra will just work its way out). Snug the cone against the bearings as with all bearings on a bike: enough to prevent side play but still allow free rotation. Replace the lock washer then use the locknut to hold everything in place. As before, expect to have to loosen the locknut and readjust the cone once or twice before attaining the best of both worlds.

▪ CHAIN RINGS AND BOTTON BRACKETS ▪

The following paragraphs are designed to step you easily through the procedures of replacing a worn-out chain ring and lubricating your bottom

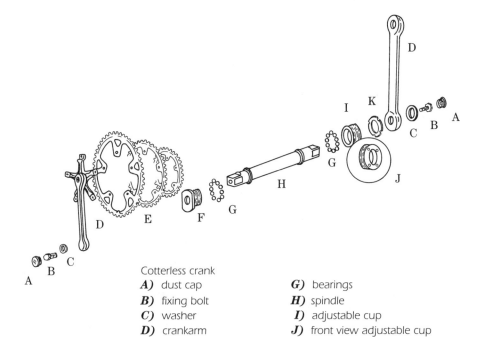

Cotterless crank

A) dust cap
B) fixing bolt
C) washer
D) crankarm
E) chainrings/chainwheels
F) fixed cup
G) bearings
H) spindle
I) adjustable cup
J) front view adjustable cup
K) lockring

Cotterless crankbolt.

Crankset closeup showing multi-piece crank, cotterless crank dustcap, and smallest of three chainrings.

bracket. Bottom bracket overhaul seems to many mountain bikers to be the equivalent of pulling a car's engine. It was, back in the days when cotter pins secured the crankarms and had to be knocked out with ball peen hammers or drilled out. Believe me, it's a relative piece-of-cake job today. And it's made even easier by my own lazy method of working entirely from the left side of the bike (reaching through the bracket for the right-side bearings), thereby not removing the chain rings and fixed cup at all.

Before we begin, don't become confused by the double names for many of the pieces involved—crankarms/cranks, chain rings/chainwheels, axle/spindle/crankshaft—or by the selective use of some terms. "Sprocket," for example, is used to refer either to chain rings or to individual cogs on the freewheel "cluster" (a word meaning the group of five to eight sprockets on the rear wheel). Yet while "cog," according to *Webster's,* can be used for any notched wheel (each notch is also called a tooth), in biking it refers almost exclusively to cluster sprockets—not the chain rings.

Chain Ring Removal and Disassembly

Begin by removing the two metal or plastic crankarm dust caps. Some are fitted for an Allen, but most have a slot that can be handled with a wide-blade screwdriver, or the side of a cone wrench, or even a quarter held by a crescent wrench or channel locks on the trail. I used to toss these things (the dust caps), thinking they were just for looks, but my Utah mechanic friends Ken Gronseth and Brad Hansen told me to knock that off. Their purpose is to keep the crank threads clean, which makes it easy to screw in the crank-removal tool.

Once these caps are out, you can see the crankarm-fixing bolts. Universal tools have heads fitted for various sizes of bolts; crank tools made specifically for one type of crank will have one end that fits the crankarm bolt and the other end beveled to accept the jaws of a large crescent or a short breaker-bar assembly to twist off the bolt. (Except for the Sugino Autex crankarm bolt-puller system, that is. The Autex employs a special heavy-duty dust cap that acts as a puller when a 6 mm Allen wrench is applied.)

But back to the more usual crank pullers. Remove the crankarm bolt (let's assume we're working with the right-chain ring side) or, in the case of "nutted assemblies" found on many bikes, the nut, and *don't* forget to remove the washer as well. Fail to pull out the washer and the next step won't work. (Crankarm bolts or nuts on both sides are removed counter-clockwise.)

With your fingers alone (so as not to strip threads), start the crankarm puller into the crankarm, then use a wrench to screw it in as far as it will go. Be sure the threads mesh perfectly.

Now insert the extractor portion—that piece that turns through the inside of the puller—into the puller body; turn it by hand until you feel its tip engage the spindle (axle) end. With a breaker bar, large crescent, or universal tool, turn the extractor clockwise; you'll see the chain ring assembly begin to slide toward you, away from and off the spindle. Lift the chain off the chain ring, place it out of the way on the bottom bracket housing, and remove the left-side crankarm in the same manner.

This is an excellent time to clean your chain rings and to make sure the chain-ring-fixing bolts—those that hold the sprockets together, located near the spider (the five metal arms radiating out from the crankarm to the attachment points for the chain rings)—are tight. By the way, it's a good idea every now and then to check that these are tight. They seldom come loose, but if they do they'll produce an untrue chain ring and cause chain rub and noise on the front derailleur cage. The individual chain rings can be separated easily by using an Allen wrench to remove these fixing bolts, and then lifting off the rings. This will be done if you are replacing a worn sprocket or altering your gear pattern. Again, be careful to dismantle and reassemble in exact order; most chainwheels have small spacer washers that must be replaced.

Bottom-Bracket Disassembly

Once the crankarms are removed, you can proceed to the bottom bracket. As I mentioned, I remove only the adjustable (left-side) cup when pulling maintenance, thereby making chains-ring removal unnecessary. You will find the fixed cup to be difficult, because it usually is nearly frozen in place and has a very thin "face" to grip with a wrench. (It must be thin to fit between the chain rings and bottom bracket.) The lock-ring/fixed-cup tool is a must. Back out the cup. (Almost all ATBs are English threaded, so when looking at the cup you will turn it clockwise for removal.)

Moving to the adjustable cup, you'll see a notched lock ring surrounding it. The lock-ring/fixed-cup tool is best for its removal, though on the road, when I'm desperate, I've used screwdrivers and the flat side of a crescent (you'll see how this could be done). In time, however, the lock ring is ruined this way; besides, you shouldn't need to mess with your bottom bracket on the road unless you've been out for a year or so, or under water for a week. Using the proper tool, engage the angled tip in a lock-ring notch and remove it—counterclockwise. Now use an adjustable cup tool to engage the pin holes (or slots) in the cup's face, and back it out completely.

If your bottom bracket is sealed, remove the seal as described in the wheel-bearing-maintenance discussion earlier, by slipping a knife blade or thin screwdriver tip beneath it and prying upward. Many nonsealed systems will have a removable plastic sheath inside, designed to shed some of the water that leaks into the frame if all frame holes have not been plugged (something that should be done immediately upon purchasing a bike and noticing a hole), and that pours into the frame if, to prevent theft, you take your saddle and seatpost with you when leaving your bike and fail to cork the hole.

The ball bearings will probably be in a retainer ring. If so, notice in which direction the retainer faces as you remove the spindle; the solid back of the retainer should face *away* from you. Also notice if one end of the spindle is

Adjustable cup removed exposing plastic sleeve.

longer than the other. Many axles today are symmetrical, but if one side is longer it will extend toward the chain rings. Clean, inspect, and if necessary replace bearings. Wipe all surfaces clean and inspect the spindle and cups for bearing wear.

Bottom-Bracket Reassembly

After thorough cleaning and close inspection, apply a generous bead of grease on the inside of your fixed cup, replace the bearings, and cover them with a second layer of grease. Thread this cup back into the frame (right side, chain ring side) with your fingers first, then by using the tool, snugging it well. To ensure easy removal months in the future, apply a bit of

Bearings repacked and liberally greased.

grease to the threads inside the bottom bracket before replacing cups. (Note that if you have not removed this fixed cup, you will have to reach through the bottom bracket, and from the right side through the spindle hole, to clean/lube/replace bearings. In my opinion that's still easier to do than messing with the fixed cup.)

Lubricate and replace the bearings in the adjustable cup in the same manner, but don't yet thread the cup into place. Take the cleaned spindle, longer side (if there is one) toward the fixed cup, and, after slipping it through the plastic sleeve, carefully guide it through the bracket and fixed cup from the left side of the bike.

Adjustable cup and adjustable cup lockring tool.

While holding the spindle by one end, pick up the adjustable cup, engage the spindle in the cup hole, and thread it into the frame a few turns. Move to the right side of the bike for a moment and replace the right-hand crankarm securely. (Do grease the bolt threads—or nut threads if you're working with a nutted assembly. Do *not* grease the crankarm hole, the portion that slides over the spindle.) Now, back on the left side, turn the adjustable cup into the frame until it is finger-tight against the bearings. Screw the lock ring onto the adjustable cup and snug it down with the lock-ring tool. Reach through the frame to grasp the right crankarm and, moving it back and forth, check for side play. (Hold the crankarm itself when doing this, not the pedal. There is too much play within most pedals for you to get a true feel for bottom-bracket side play.) If it's too loose, as it probably will be, back off the lock ring a bit, tighten the adjustable cup slightly, then retighten the lock ring. Remember the technique you learned in other bearing work throughout the bike: You are looking for the best possible combination of no side play and free spindle rotation.

When the adjustment seems correct, replace the left-side crankarm and check again for your adjustment. Place the arms at both the six/twelve o'clock and three/nine o'clock positions when doing this. Have patience. Get it right.

Reinstall the dust caps and restore the chain to the chain ring. Check the tightness of these fixing bolts once a week for the next few months. If they haven't worked free by then, they're not going to.

▪ SUSPENSION FORKS ▪

I can't equip my own bike with a suspension fork due to the occasional need to hang two fully loaded panniers alongside the front wheel (which makes four panniers total and between sixty and eighty pounds on my weeks-long backcountry mountain bike treks), but that hasn't kept me from testing and enjoying suspension forks. What it has kept me from is learning how to maintain them on the trails, and so I turned to one of the experts—master mechanic Ken Gronseth—when it came time to add a few forked words. I thank him kindly for his help, and Cannondale for permission to copy their drawing and instruction.

Suspension forks are no longer an exotic aftermarket item. They are now standard equipment at almost all price levels of mountain bikes. All suspension forks consist of some kind of spring mechanism to absorb and

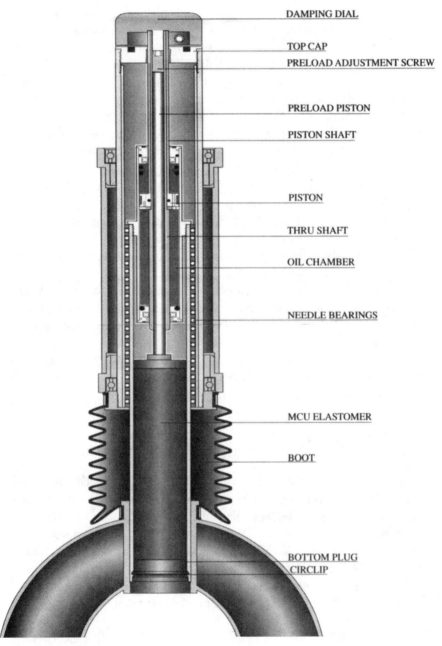

DAMPING DIAL

TOP CAP
PRELOAD ADJUSTMENT SCREW

PRELOAD PISTON

PISTON SHAFT

PISTON

THRU SHAFT

OIL CHAMBER

NEEDLE BEARINGS

MCU ELASTOMER

BOOT

BOTTOM PLUG
CIRCLIP

Suspension Fork diagram

rebound the energy of a bump, and a damping mechanism to control the rate of absorption and rebound. Aside from some bikes where these mechanisms are contained in the head tube of the bike, the majority of fork designs share several common design features: (1) The fork crown clamps around the upper fork tubes; (2) the upper fork tubes telescope in and out of lower fork tubes, which are joined together by a brake bridge; (3) the spring and damping mechanisms are contained inside the upper/lower tube assemblies.

Suspension forks can be grouped into three general categories by their type of spring and damping mechanisms. *Air/oil forks* use a chamber of compressed air as the spring, plus a chamber where oil moves through a valving circuit to control the damping rate. *Spring or elastomer forks* use a metal coil spring or a stack of elastomer (polyurethane elastopolymer) doughnuts as the spring. (Damping in a coil spring fork is controlled by a piece of elastomer placed in tandem with the spring. Damping in an elastomer fork is controlled by elastomer doughnuts alone.) Most recent are the *hybrid forks* combining the best properties of the first two types. Hybrid forks use a stack of microcellular foam doughnuts as the spring. Damping is controlled by a seated oil cartridge placed in one fork leg.

Because each brand of fork is unique in its parts and construction, it is beyond the scope of this book to provide specific repair instructions. To make matters more complicated, suspension fork design is still evolving rapidly; each season brings new forks into the shop. However, I'll provide some general inspection and service tips, but first a quick word for those of you attempting more detailed repair.

Air/oil forks are the most complicated in terms of number of parts and the specialty tools needed to work on them. Elastomer and hybrid forks have fewer parts and require few if any specialty tools. Before attempting to adjust or work on your suspension fork, read and understand the service manual for your particular fork. If you're comfortable overhauling the bottom bracket on your bike, you should have enough expertise to overhaul an elastomer or hybrid fork, or to do an oil change on an air/oil fork. But follow your service manual instructions *carefully.*

Inspection/General Service

Inspect your suspension fork before each ride. The front wheel should be centered between the fork blades. If you are installing a new tire, make sure there is at least a quarter inch of clearance between the top of the tire and the bottom of the brake bridge when the fork is fully compressed. Assuming the front wheel is true, an off-center wheel is commonly caused by one of the upper fork tubes being positioned higher than the other in the fork crown clamps. The clamping bolts holding one or both upper fork tubes may have to be loosened in order to reposition the tubes properly. The bolts connecting the brake bridge to the lower fork tubes may also have to be loosened if the fork legs are extremely misaligned. It will be necessary to have access to a torque wrench (measuring applied torque in inch-pounds) to tighten the bolts to the manufacturer's specs. Overtightening the fork crown bolts can ovalize the upper fork legs, which will interfere with smooth fork operation. In addition, overtightening can easily lead to stripped bolts.

Next, push down on the handlebars and unweight them quickly. The fork should respond smoothly. Less-than-smooth operation may be caused by: (1) Low air pressure in air/oil forks. The pressure should be checked every few weeks. Also, look for oil leaks at the seal between the upper and lower fork tubes. If the fork won't hold air pressure, or if there is an oil leak, a bike shop with specialty tools will be needed to service the fork. (2) Excessive friction between the upper and lower fork tubes in elastomer or hybrid forks. This can be caused by water or dirt entering the forks, or by normal wear over a season or two. These forks need to be disassembled and the internal parts cleaned and greased. All types of forks can benefit from accordion-style boots that cover the joint between the upper and lower fork tubes; these keep dirt from contaminating the inside of the fork.

Finally, check the amount of play between the upper and lower fork tubes. Excessive play can sometimes feel like a loose headset under hard braking. Make sure the headset is properly adjusted. Then, with the front of the bike off the ground, grasp the fork crown in one hand and wiggle the lower fork tubes to feel for play. Excessive play means that the bushings inside the fork (which allow the upper and lower tubes to slide past one another) are worn. Air/oil forks will need to be serviced by the dealer to correct this problem. Many elastomer and hybrid forks can be serviced by the rider.

GLOSSARY

This short list does not contain all the terms used by mountain bikers on the trails. But there's enough of the lingo here to help you start communicating with the natives.

ATB: All-terrain bike. This, like "fat-tire bike," is another name for a mountain bike.

Bladed: Refers to a dirt road that has been smoothed out by the use of a wide blade on earth-moving equipment. "Blading" gets rid of the teeth-chattering, much-cursed washboards found on so many dirt roads after heavy vehicle use.

Blaze: A mark on a tree made by chipping away a piece of the bark, usually done to designate a trail. Such trails are sometimes described as "blazed." *See* **Signed.**

BLM: Bureau of Land Management, an agency of the federal government.

Buffed: Used to describe a very smooth trail.

Catching air: Taking a jump in such a way that both wheels of the bike are off the ground at the same time.

Clean: Used most often as a verb to denote the action of pedaling a tough section of trail successfully.

Dab: To touch the ground with a foot or hand in order to stay upright while trail riding.

Deadfall: A tangled mass of fallen trees or branches.

Diversion ditch: A usually narrow, shallow ditch dug across or around a trail.

Funneling the water in this manner keeps it from destroying the trail.

Double-track: The dual tracks made by a jeep or other vehicle, with grass or weeds or rock between. You can ride in either of these tracks, but you will of course find that whichever one you choose, and no matter how many times you change back and forth, the other track will appear to offer smoother travel.

Dugway: A steep, unpaved, switchbacked descent.

Endo: Flipping end over end (that is, *you* flipping end over end, along with your bike for at least part of the flip). This is not a suggested trail-riding technique.

Feathering: Using a light touch on the brake lever, hitting it lightly many times rather than very hard or locking the brake.

Four-wheel-drive: Any vehicle with drive-wheel capability on all four wheels (a jeep, for instance, has four-wheel drive, as compared with a two-wheel-drive passenger car). Also, a rough road or trail that requires four-wheel-drive capability (or a one-wheel-drive mountain bike!) to negotiate it.

Game trail: The usually narrow trail made by deer, elk, or other game.

Gated: A trail described as *gated* simply has a gate across it. Don't forget that the rule is if you find a gate closed, close it behind you; if you find one open, leave it that way.

Giardia: One real bad disease, contracted from impure water sources. See page 123 for water purification techniques and more about this nasty ailment.

Gnarly: A term thankfully used less and less these days, referring to tough trails.

Hammer: To ride very hard.

Hardpack: A trail in which the dirt surface is packed down hard. Such trails make for good and fast riding, and very painful landings. Bikers most often use *hardpack* as both a noun and an adjective, and *hard-packed* as an adjective only.

Hike-a-bike: What you do when the road or trail becomes too steep or rough to remain in the saddle.

Jeep road, jeep trail: A rough road or trail passable only with four-wheel-drive capability (or mountain bike).

Kamikaze: Applied to the idiot mountain bikers who scream down hiking trails, endangering the physical and mental safety of the walking, biking, and equestrian traffic they meet.

Multipurpose land: A BLM designation of land that is open to many uses; mountain biking is allowed.

ORV: A motorized off-road vehicle.

Out-and-back trail: A ride in which you will return on the same trail you pedaled out. While this might sound far more boring than a loop route, many trails look very different when pedaled in the opposite direction.

Pack stock: Horses, mules, llamas, et cetera, carrying provisions along the trails.

Portage: To carry your bike on your person.

Quads: The extensor muscle in the front of the thigh (which is separated into four parts). Also, USGS maps.

Runoff: Rainwater or snowmelt.

Scree: An accumulation of loose stones or rocky debris lying on a slope or at the base of a hill or cliff.

Signed: A *signed* trail has signs in place of blazes.

Single-track: A single, narrow path through grass or brush or over rocky terrain, often created by deer, elk, or backpackers. Single-track riding is some of the best fun around.

Slickrock: The rock-hard, compacted sandstone that's great to ride and even prettier to look at. You'll appreciate it even more if you think of it as a petrified sand dune or seabed (which it is), and if the rider before you hasn't left tire marks (from unnecessary skidding) or granola bar wrappers behind.

Snowmelt: Runoff produced by the melting of snow.

Snowpack: Unmelted snow accumulated during weeks or months of winter—or over years, in high-mountain terrain.

Spur: A road or trail that intersects the main trail you're following.

Switchback: A zigzagging road or trail designed to assist in traversing steep terrain. Mountain bikers should *not* skid through switchbacks on a descent, no matter how much fun it is or how happy they are to have made it up the other side.

Technical: Terrain that is difficult to ride due not to its grade (steepness) but to its obstacles—rocks, logs, ledges, loose soil, for example.

Topo: Short for topographical map, the kind that shows both linear distance and elevation gain and loss; *topo* is pronounced with both vowels long.

Trashed: A trail that has been destroyed (same term used no matter what has destroyed it—cattle, horses, or even mountain bikers riding when the ground was too wet).

Two-wheel-drive: This refers to any vehicle with drive-wheel capability on only two wheels (a passenger car, for instance, has two-wheel drive); a two-wheel-drive road is a road or trail easily traveled by an ordinary car.

Washboarded: Describes a road that is surfaced with many ridges spaced closely together, like the ripples on a washboard. These make for very rough riding, and even worse driving in a car or jeep.

Water bar: An earth, rock, or wooden structure that funnels water off trails to reduce erosion.

Whoop-de-do: Closely spaced dips or undulations in a trail. These are often encountered in areas traveled heavily by ORVs.

Wilderness area: Land that is officially set aside by the federal government to remain *natural*—pure, pristine, and uncontaminated by any vehicle, including mountain bikes. Though mountain bikes had not been born in 1964 (when the U.S. Congress passed the Wilderness Act, establishing the National Wilderness Preservation system), they are considered a form of mechanical transport and are thereby excluded; in short, stay out—or *hike* in without your bike.

Wind-chill: A reference to the wind's cooling effect upon exposed flesh. For example, if the temperature is 10 degrees F and the wind is blowing at 20 miles per hour, the wind-chill (that is, the actual temperature to which your skin reacts) is minus 32 degrees. If you're riding in wet conditions, things are even worse—the wind-chill would then be *minus 74 degrees!*

Windfall: Anything (trees, limbs, brush, fellow bikers) blown down by the wind.

Note: This glossary is adapted from the *Dennis Coello's America by Mountain Bike Series* of nationwide trail guides.

GEAR CHART FOR 26-INCH WHEEL

Number of teeth in front sprocket

	22	24	26	28	30	32	34	36	38	40	42	44	46	48	50	52
12	47.7	52	56.3	60.7	65	69.3	73.4	78	82.3	86.7	91	95.3	99.7	104	108.3	112.7
13	44	48	52	56	60	64	68	72	76	80	84	88	92	96	100	104
14	40.9	44.6	48.3	52	55.8	59.4	63.1	66.9	70.6	74.3	78	81.7	85.4	89.1	92.9	96.6
15	38.1	41.6	45.1	48.5	52	55.5	58.9	62.4	65.9	69.3	72.8	76.3	79.7	83.2	86.7	90.1
16	35.8	39	42.3	45.5	48.8	52	55.3	58.5	61.8	65	68.3	71.5	74.8	78	81.3	84.5
17	33.6	36.7	39.8	42.8	45.9	48.9	52	55.1	58.1	61.2	64.2	67.3	70.4	73.4	76.5	79.5
18	31.8	34.7	37.6	40.4	43.3	46.2	49.1	52	54.9	57.8	60.7	63.6	66.4	69.3	72.2	75.1
19	30.1	32.8	35.6	38.3	41.1	43.8	46.5	49.3	52	54.7	57.8	60.2	62.9	65.7	68.4	71.2
20	28.6	31.2	33.8	36.4	39	41.6	44.2	46.8	49.4	52	54.6	57.2	59.8	62.4	65	67.6
21	27.2	29.7	32.2	34.7	37.1	39.6	42.1	44.6	47	49.5	52	54.5	57	59.4	61.9	63.4
22	26	28.4	30.7	33.1	35.5	37.8	40.2	42.5	44.9	47.3	49.6	52	54.4	56.7	59.1	61.5
23	24.9	27.1	29.4	31.7	33.9	36.2	38.4	40.7	43	45.2	47.5	49.7	52	54.3	56.5	58.8
24	23.8	26	28.2	30.3	32.5	34.7	36.8	39	41.2	43.3	45.5	47.7	49.8	52	54.2	56.3
25	22.9	25	27	29.1	31.2	33.3	35.4	37.4	39.5	41.6	43.7	45.8	47.8	49.9	52	54.1
26	22	24	26	28	30	32	34	36	38	40	42	44	46	48	50	52
27	21.2	23.1	25	27	28.9	30.8	32.7	34.7	36.6	38.5	40.4	42.4	44.3	46.2	48.1	50.1
28	20.4	22.3	24.1	26	27.9	29.7	31.6	33.4	35.3	37.1	39	40.9	42.7	44.6	46.4	48.3
29	19.7	21.5	23.3	25.1	26.9	28.7	30.5	32.3	34.1	35.9	37.7	39.4	41.2	43	44.8	46.6
30	19.1	20.8	22.5	24.3	26	27.7	29.5	31.2	32.9	34.7	36.4	38.1	39.9	41.6	43.3	45.1
31	18.5	20.1	21.8	23.5	25.2	26.8	28.5	30.2	31.9	33.5	35.2	36.9	38.6	40.3	41.9	43.6
32	17.9	19.5	21.1	22.8	24.4	26	27.6	29.3	30.9	32.5	34.1	35.8	37.4	39	40.6	42.3
33	17.3	18.9	20.5	22.1	23.6	25.2	26.7	28.4	29.9	31.5	33.1	34.7	36.2	37.8	39.4	41
34	16.8	18.4	19.9	21.4	22.9	24.5	26	27.5	29.1	30.6	32.1	33.6	35.2	36.7	38.2	39.8

Number of teeth in front sprocket

inch gear= $\dfrac{\text{\# teeth in front sprocket}}{\text{\# teeth in rear sprocket}}$ × wheel diameter in inches

Example: $\dfrac{48}{13}$ × 26 = 96 inch gear

(Compute linear distance traveled with each crank rotation by multiplying "inch gear" by pi = 3.14)

Example: 96 × 3.14 = 301.44" (or 25.12' linear distance)

Some people contend that the higher profile tires on 26" mountain bike wheels makes them virtually the same, as far as gear ratios are concerned, as 27" thin tires. I have measured the difference, computed it over the length of several day rides or a single weekend tour, and cannot agree.

INTERNATIONAL MOUNTAIN BICYCLING ASSOCIATION (IMBA'S) RULES OF THE TRAIL

1. Ride on open trails only. Respect trail and road closures (ask if not sure), avoid possible trespass on private land, obtain permits and authorization as may be required. Federal and State wilderness areas are closed to cycling.

2. Leave no trace. Be sensitive to the dirt beneath you. Even on open trails, you should not ride under conditions where you will leave evidence of your passing, such as on certain soils shortly after rain. Observe the different types of soils and trail construction; practice low-impact cycling. This also means staying on the trail and not creating new ones. Be sure to pack out at least as much as you pack in.

3. Control your bicycle. Inattention for even a second can cause a disaster. Excessive speed can maim and threaten people; there is no excuse for it.

4. Always yield the trail. Make known your approach well in advance. A friendly greeting (or a bell) is considerate and works well; startling someone may cause loss of trail access. Show your respect when passing others by slowing to a walk or even stopping. Anticipate that other trail users may be around corners or in blind spots.

5. Never spook animals. All animals are startled by an unannounced approach, a sudden movement, or a loud noise. This can be dangerous for you, for others, and for the animals. Give animals extra room

and time to adjust to you. In passing, use special care and follow the directions of horseback riders (ask if uncertain). Running cattle and disturbing wild animals are serious offenses. Leave gates as you found them, or as marked.

6. Plan ahead. Know your equipment, your ability, and the area in which you are riding and prepare accordingly. Be self-sufficient at all times. Wear a helmet, keep your machine in good condition, and carry necessary supplies for changes in weather and other conditions. A well-executed trip is a satisfaction to you and not a burden or offense to others.

For more information, contact IMBA, P.O. Box 412043, Los Angeles, CA 90041; 818-792-8830.

MOUNTAIN BIKE AND CYCLING ORGANIZATIONS

Adventure Cycling Association
P.O. Box 8308
Missoula, MT 59807

**International Mountain
Association (IMBA)**
P.O. Box 412043
Los Angeles, CA 90041
818-792-8830

League of American Bicyclists
190 West Ostend Street, Suite 120
Baltimore, MD 21230
301-539-3399

**National Off-Road Bicycle
Association (NORBA)**
One Olympic Plaza
Colorado Springs, CO 80909
719-578-4596

Rails-to-Trails Conservancy
1400 16th Street NW, Suite 300
Washington, DC 20036
202-797-5400

> Note: There are hundreds of state and local bicycle clubs and organizations. All of them can be located through the national organizations listed above.

CANADA

Alberta Bicycle Association
Percy Page Centre
11759 Groat Road
Edmonton, Alberta T5M 3K6
403-453-8518

Bicycle Nova Scotia
P.O. Box 3010 South
Halifax, Nova Scotia B3J 3G6
902-477-9804

Canadian Cycling Association
1600 James Naismith Drive
Gloucester, Ontario K1B 5N4
613-748-5629

**Canadian Mountain Bike
Polo Association**
Blackcomb Mountain
4545 Blackcomb Way
Box 98
Whistler, B.C. V0N 1B0
604-932-3141

Cycling Association of Yukon
P.O. Box 5082
Whitehorse, Yukon Y1A 453

Cycling B.C.
1367 W. Broadway, Suite 332
Vancouver, B.C. V6H 4A9
604-737-3034

Cycling New Brunswick
457 Charterville Road
Dieppe, New Brunswick E1A 5H1
506-852-7813

Great Canadian Bicycle Rally Inc.
Box 21045
Paris, Ontario N3L 2C9
519-442-6235

Manitoba Cycling Association
200 Main Street
Winnipeg, Manitoba R3C 4M2
204-985-4055

**Newfoundland and Labrador
  Cycling Association**
P.O. Box 2127, Station C
St. John's, Newfoundland A1C 5R6
709-745-1034

Ontario Cycling Association
Ontario Sports and Recreation
  Building
1185 Egglington Avenue, East
North York, Ontario M3C 3C6
416-426-7242

Saskatchewan Cycling Association
2205 Victoria Avenue
Regina, Saskatchewan S4P 0S4
306-780-9200

Tourism PEI
Visitor Services Division
P.O. Box 940
Charlottetown, Prince
  Edward Island
Canada C1A 7M5
800-463-4734
[Specific request for cycling
information must be made,
or caller will receive only
a standard tourist package.]

Toronto Bicycling Network
131 Bloor Street West
Suite 200, Box 279
Toronto, Ontario M5S 1R8
416-766-1985

Vancouver Bicycle Club
P.O. Box 2235
Vancouver, B.C. V6B 3W2
604-731-4831

Velo Falifax Bicycle Club
Box 125
Dartmouth, Nova Scotia B2Y 3Y2

MAGAZINES DEDICATED TO OR INCLUDING MOUNTAIN BIKES

Adventure Cyclist
P.O. Box 8308
Missoula, MT 59807
406-721-1776

Bicycling
33 East Minor Street
Emmaus, PA 18049
610-967-5171

BIKE
Box 1028
Dana Point, CA 92629
714-496-5922

Dirt Rag
AKA Productions
5732 Third Street
Verona, PA 15147
412-795-7495

Mountain Bike
6420 Wilshire Boulevard
Los Angeles, CA 90048
213-782-2372 (fax only)

Mountain Bike Action
10600 Sepulveda Boulevard
Mission Hills, CA 91345
818-365-6831

Mountain Biking
7950 Deering Avenue
Canoga Park, CA 91304
800-562-9182

NORBA News
NORBA National Headquarters
One Olympic Plaza
Colorado Springs, CA 80909
719-578-4596

APPENDIX E

TOURING COMPANIES

There are hundreds of touring companies. The ones listed below are not the only good ones out there, but they're the ones I've toured with in the past and with whom I would do so again—in a minute. It's tough work to put on a good tour and I'm privileged to have had an inside look at what makes them tick. So call up, sign up, and begin counting the days. No matter where you choose to ride, you'll have a ball.

Adventure Cycling Association
P.O. Box 8308
Missoula, MT 59807
406-721-1776

Backcountry Bicycle Tours
P.O. Box 4229
Bozeman, MT 59772
406-586-3556

Backroads
1516 Fifth Street
Berkeley, CA 94710
800-462-2848

Bike Vermont, Inc.
P.O. Box 207
Woodstock, VT 05091
802-457-3553; 800-257-2226

Butterfield & Robinson
70 Bond Street
Toronto, Ontario M5B 1X3
Canada
416-864-1354
800-387-1147 (from U.S.)
800-268-8415 (from Canada)

Pack and Paddle
601 E. Pinhook Road
Lafayette, LA 70501
318-232-5854

Progressive Travels
224 West Galer Avenue, Suite C
Seattle, WA 98119
800-245-2229

Rim Tours
94 West 1st North
Moab, UT 84532
800-626-7335

Road Less Traveled
P.O. Box 8187
Longmont, CO 80501
303-678-8750

Vermont Bicycle Touring (VBT)
P.O. Box 711
Bristol, VT 05443
802-453-4811; 800-245-3868

Western Spirit Cycling
P.O. Box 411
Moab, UT 84532
801-259-8732; 800-845-BIKE

And there's one more to add, a brand new company unlike any I'd ever pedaled with before. Its mountain bike rides are operated out of a lovely inn in Vermont's Green Mountains, and if you don't feel like pedaling or if it's raining, you can read and sip cider in the beautiful place or choose to be shuttled off to canoe or practice archery for the day. Contact:

The Great Outdoors Adventure
   Bike Tours
219 Woodstock Avenue
Rutland, VT 05701
800-345-5182

PANNIER MANUFACTURERS

Bell Sports/Blackburn
160 Knowles Drive
Los Gatos, CA 95030
408-370-1010; 800-776-5677

Bike Pro USA
3701 West Roanoke
Phoenix, AZ 85009
602-272-3588
800-338-7581; 800-442-8900

Bushwhacker USA
P.O. Box 297
Morgan, UT 84050
801-829-6801; 800-343-1256

Cannondale
9 Brookside Place
Georgetown, CT 06829
203-544-9800; 203-544-3311

CyclePro
22710 72nd Avenue South
Kent, WA 98032
206-395-1100; 800-222-5527

Eclipse
3771 E. Ellsworth Road
Ann Arbor, MI 48108
800-666-1500

Global Design Lab
23555 Telo Avenue
Torrance, CA 90505
310-539-6146

Hypersport
120 West Maine Street, #203
West Dundee, IL 60118
708-551-9945; 800-566-HYPE

Jandd Mountaineering
30 South Salsipuedes Street
Santa Barbara, CA 93103
805-564-2044

Kangaroo Baggs
P.O. Box 1870
#6 St. Francis Plaza
Ranchos de Taos, NM 87557
505-751-7389; 505-751-7433

Leader Sports Products
43 North Country Shopping
    Center
Plattsburg, NY 12901
518-562-1653

Lone Peak
3474 South 2300 East
Salt Lake City, UT 84109
801-272-5217; 800-777-7679

Louis Garneau USA
66 Main Street
Box 755
Newport, VT 05855
802-334-5885; 800-448-1984

Madden USA
2400 Central Avenue
Boulder, CO 80301
303-442-5828

McEnroe Brothers
P.O. Box 1170
New Seabury, MA 02649
508-564-5146; 800-433-6863

Mountainsmith Cycling Gear
18301 West Colfax Avenue
Building P
Golden, CO 80401
303-279-5930

Ortlieb/PMI
P.O. Box 803
Lafayotte, GA 30728
706-764-1437; 800-282-7673

Overland Equipment
2145 Park Avenue, Suite 4
Chico, CA 95928
916-894-5605; 800-487-8851

**Richard Jones Convertible
  Backpacks**
P.O. Box 919
Fort Collins, CO 80522-0919
303-484-7562
(panniers convert to backpacks)

Robert Beckman Designs
P.O. Box 6952
Bend, OR 97708
503-388-5146

Schwinn Cycling and Fitness
1690 38th Street
Boulder, CO 80301
303-939-0100

SOURCES AND PRODUCTS MENTIONED IN TEXT

Bike Nashbar Catalog
4111 Simon Road
Youngstown, OH 44512
800-627-4227

BlackBottoms
P.O. Box 7104
Salt Lake City, UT 84107
801-262-6503; 800-445-3640

B.O.B. Trailers
3641 Sacramento Drive, #3
San Luis Obispo, CA 93401
805-541-2554

Bruce Gordon Cycles (and racks)
613 Second Street
Petaluma, CA 94952
707-762-5601

CamelBak/FasTrak Systems, Inc.
P.O. Box 1029
Weatherford, TX 76086
817-594-1000

Campmor Catalog
P.O. Box 700-G
Saddle River, NJ 07458
800-226-7667

Cascade Designs
4000 1st Avenue South
Seattle, WA 98134
800-527-1527

Chums, Ltd.
P.O. Box 950
Hurricane, UT 84737
800-323-3707

Coleman Peak 1 Outdoor Equipment
3600 North Hydraulic
Wichita, KS 67219
800-835-3278

Crash Pack/Slide Zone, Inc.
P.O. Box 781572
San Antonio, TX 78278
210-344-3935; 800-754-3305

CycleAware, Inc.
323 Spreckels Drive, Suite F
Aptos, CA 95003
408-685-1115

CycoActive Products
117 East Louisa Street
Seattle, WA 98102
206-323-2349

Duckbill Visors
P.O. Box 3364
Santa Cruz, CA 95063
408-423-2030

**Excel Sports Boulder
  Mail Order Catalog**
800-627-6664

Gator
3789 South 300 West, Building C
Salt Lake City, UT 84115
801-261-3729; 800-325-3729

Headland Bicycle Accessories
537 South 48th Street, #102
Tempe, AZ 85281
602-858-0006; 800-683-2925

Incredibell
Mirrycle Corporation
6101 Ben Place
Boulder, CO 80301
303-442-3495

Innovations in Cycling
2700 East Bilby Road, Building C
Tucson, AZ 85706
602-295-3936

Kroops Goggles
9865-E North Washington
  Boulevard
Laurel, MD 20707
301-498-5848

Kryptonite Corporation
320 Turnpike Street
Canton, MA 02021
617-828-6655

MARWI USA
Night Pro Lights
1 Union Drive
Olney, IL 62450
618-395-8471

Mountain Mirrycle
(see Incredibell; same company)

O'Neil's Mail-Order Catalog
800-638-6344

Outdoor Research
1000 1st Avenue South
Seattle, WA 98134
206-467-8197; 800-421-2421

Patagonia Mail Order, Inc.
1609 West Babcock Street
P.O. Box 8900
Bozeman, MT 59715
800-638-6464

Pearl Izumi
2300 Central Avenue, #G
Boulder, CO 80301
303-938-1700

SOURCES AND PRODUCTS MENTIONED IN TEXT

Performance Bicycle Catalog
800-727-2453

REI Mail-Order Catalog
800-426-4840

Seat Locker

These locks are now distributed by Avenir, and should be available in many well-stocked bike shops. If you can't find one, ask your bike shop dealer to call Avenir at 800-776-7641 to order one for you, and look for them in the bike catalogs.

Sierra Trading Post
5025 Campstool Road
Cheyenne, WY 82007
307-775-8000

The Bike Club
Winner International
800-CLUB-321

Vagabond Outfitters, Inc.
288-18th Avenue
San Francisco, CA 94121
800-492-8434

Vasque Outdoor Footwear
314 Main Street
Red Wing, MN 55066
612-388-8211

Roly Caps
730 West 400 North
Salt Lake City, UT 84116
801-261-5313

Vetta
800-GO-VETTA

VistaLite
800-456-BELL

VO2 MAX, Inc.
Pyro Pedals
16372 Skyliners Road
Bend, OR 97701
503-389-9849; 800-927-7976

Wiggy's
2482 Industrial Boulevard
P.O. Box 2124
Grand Junction, CO 81502
970-241-6465; 800-748-1827

TRAIL INFORMATION SOURCES

Adventure Cycling Association
P.O. Box 8308
Missoula, MT 59807
406-721-1776

Bureau of Land Management (BLM)
U.S. Department of the Interior
18th and "C" Streets, N.W., Room 1013
Washington, DC 20240

Canadian Cycling Association
1600 James Naismith Drive
Gloucester, Ontario K1B 5N4
Canada
613-748-5629

Dennis Coello's America by Mountain Bike Series
800-247-9437

International Mountain Bicycling Association (IMBA)
P.O. Box 412043
Los Angeles, CA 90041
818-792-8830

League of American Bicyclists
190 West Ostend Street, Suite 120
Baltimore, MD 21230
301-539-3399

National Forests and Wilderness Areas
Forest Service
U.S. Department of Agriculture
12th and Independence Streets, S.W.
P.O. Box 2417
Washington, DC 20013

> Note: Remember that mountain bikes are not allowed in designated Wilderness areas.

**National Off-Road Bicycling
Association (NORBA)**
One Olympic Plaza
Colorado Springs, CO 80909
719-578-4596

Rails-to-Trails Conservancy
1400 16th Street, N.W., Suite 300
Washington, DC 20036
202-797-5400

Trails Illustrated
P.O. Box 3610
Evergreen, CO 80439
800-962-1643

USGS Map Sales
Box 25286
Denver, CO 80225

INDEX